THE JOY OF ANSWERED
PRAYER

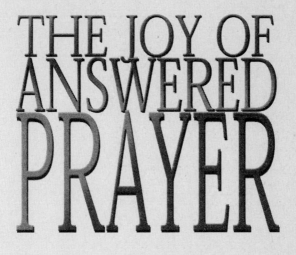

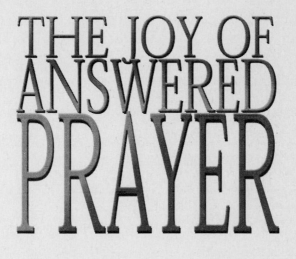

THE JOY OF ANSWERED PRAYER

D L MOODY

W

WHITAKER
HOUSE

All Scripture quotations are from the King James Version (KJV) of the Bible.

Editor's note: This book has been edited for the modern reader. Words, expressions, and sentence structure have been updated for clarity and readability.

THE JOY OF ANSWERED PRAYER
(originally published as *Prevailing Prayer*)

ISBN: 0-88368-411-X
Printed in the United States of America
© 1997 by Whitaker House

Whitaker House
30 Hunt Valley Circle
New Kensington, PA 15068

Library of Congress Cataloging-in-Publication Data

  Moody, Dwight Lyman, 1837–1899.
   The joy of answered prayer / by D. L. Moody.
     p. cm.
  Originally published: 1997.
   ISBN 0-88368-411-X (pbk.)
   1. Prayer—Christianity. I. Title.
  BV220 .M66 2002
  248.3'2—dc21

                        2002003725

1 2 3 4 5 6 7 8 9 10 11 / 10 09 08 07 06 05 04 03 02

Contents

Prayer

Prayer was appointed to convey
    The blessings God designs to give;
Long as they live should Christians pray,
    For only while they pray they live.

And shall we in dead silence lie,
    When Christ stands waiting for our prayer?
My soul, thou hast a Friend on high;
    Arise and try thy interest there.

If pain afflict, or wrongs oppress;
    If cares distract, or fears dismay;
If guilt deject, if sin distress;
    The remedy's before thee—Pray!

Depend on Christ, thou canst not fail;
    Make all thy wants and wishes known.
Fear not; His merits must prevail;
    Ask what thou wilt; it shall be done!

—Joseph Hart

CHAPTER 1

The Prayers of
the Bible

Those who have left the deepest impression on this sin-cursed earth have been men and women of prayer. You will find that prayer has been the mighty power that has moved not only God, but man also. Abraham was a man of prayer, and angels came down from heaven to converse with him. Jacob's prayer was answered in the wonderful interview at Peniel, which resulted in his having such a mighty blessing, and in softening the heart of his brother Esau. (See Genesis 32:24–30; 33:4.) The child Samuel was given in answer to Hannah's prayer. (See 1 Samuel 1:9–11, 20.) Elijah's prayer closed up the heavens for three years and six months, and he prayed again and the heavens gave rain. (See 1 Kings 17:1; 18:41–45, and James 5:17–18.)

The apostle James tells us that the prophet Elijah was a man *"subject to like passions as we are"* (James 5:17). I am thankful that those men and women who were so mighty in prayer were just like us. We are apt to think that those prophets and mighty men and women of old were different from what we are. To be sure, they lived in a much darker age, but they were *"subject to like passions."*

We read that, on another occasion, Elijah brought fire down on Mount Carmel. (See 1 Kings 18:17–39.) The prophets of Baal cried long and loud, but no answer came. The God of Elijah heard and answered his prayer. Let us remember that the God of Elijah still lives. The prophet was translated and went up to heaven (see 2 Kings 2:11), but his God still lives. We, therefore, have the same access to Him that Elijah had. We have the same warrant to go to God and ask that fire from heaven come down and consume our lusts and passions, burning up our dross and letting Christ shine through us.

Elisha prayed, and life came back to a dead child. (See 2 Kings 4:27–37.) Many of our children are *"dead in trespasses and sins"* (Eph. 2:1). Let us do as Elisha did; let us entreat God to raise them up in answer to our prayers.

Manasseh, the king, was a wicked man, and he had done everything he could against the God of his father; yet, in Babylon, when he cried to God, his cry was heard, and he was taken out of prison and put on the throne at Jerusalem. (See 2 Chronicles 33:1–2, 11–13.) Surely if God gave heed to the prayer of wicked Manasseh, He will hear ours in the time of our distress. Is this not a time of distress with a great number of our fellowmen? Are there not many among us whose hearts are burdened? As we go to the throne of grace, let us always remember that God answers prayer.

Look now at Samson. He prayed, and his strength came back, so that he slew more at his death than during his life. (See Judges 16:28–30.) He was a restored backslider, and he had power with God. If those who have been backsliders will only return to God, they will see how quickly God will answer prayer.

Job prayed, and his captivity was turned. Light came in the place of darkness, and God lifted him up above the height of his former prosperity—in answer to prayer. (See Job 42:10.)

Daniel prayed to God, and Gabriel came to tell him that he was a man greatly beloved of God. Three times that message came to him from heaven in answer to prayer. (See Daniel 9:23; 10:11, 19.) The secrets of heaven were imparted to him, and he was told that God's Son was going to be cut off for the sins of His people. (See Daniel 9:26.)

We find also that Cornelius prayed, and Peter was sent to give him the message whereby he and his household would be saved. (See Acts 10:30–33, 44.) It was in answer to prayer that this great blessing came upon Cornelius and his household. Peter had also prayed. He had gone up to the housetop to pray in the afternoon, when he had that wonderful vision of the sheet descending from heaven. (See Acts 10:9–16.) Further, it was when Christians prayed for Peter without ceasing that the angel was sent to deliver him. (See Acts 12:5–11.)

All through the Scriptures you will find that when believing prayer went up to God, the answer came down. I think it would be a very interesting study to go right through the Bible and see what has happened while God's people have been on their knees calling upon Him. Certainly the study would greatly strengthen our faith, for it would show how wonderfully the Lord has heard and delivered those who have cried out to Him for help.

Look at Paul and Silas in the prison at Philippi. As they prayed and sang praises, the place was shaken, and the jailer was converted. (See Acts 16:25–33.) Probably that one conversion has done more than any other recorded in the Bible to bring people into the kingdom of God. How many have been blessed in seeking to answer the question, *"What must I do to be saved?"* (Acts 16:30)! It was the prayer of those two godly men that brought the jailer to his knees and brought blessing to him and his family.

You remember how Stephen, as he prayed, looked up, saw the heavens opened, and saw the Son of Man at the right hand of God. (See Acts 7:55–56.) The light of heaven fell on his face so that it shone. (See Acts 6:15.) Remember, too, how the face of Moses shone as he came down from the Mount; he had been in communion with God. (See Exodus 34:29.) When we really get into communion with God, He lifts up His countenance upon us (Num. 6:26); and instead of having gloomy looks, our faces shine, because God has heard and answered our prayers.

I want to call special attention to Christ as an example for us in all things, in nothing more than in prayer. We read that Christ prayed to His Father for everything. Every great crisis in His life was preceded by prayer. Let me point out a few passages.

I never noticed until a few years ago that Christ was praying at His baptism. As He prayed, the heaven was opened, and the Holy Spirit descended on Him. (See Luke 3:21–22.) Another great event in His life was His Transfiguration. *"As he prayed, the fashion of his countenance was altered, and his raiment was white and glistering"* (Luke 9:29).

We also read this about Christ: *"It came to pass in those days, that he went out into a mountain to pray, and continued all night in prayer to God"* (Luke 6:12). This is the only place where it is recorded that the Savior spent a whole night in prayer. What was about to take place? When He came down from the mountain, He gathered His disciples around Him and preached that great discourse known as the Sermon on the Mount, the most wonderful sermon that has ever been preached to mortal men. Probably no sermon has done so much good, and it was preceded by a night of prayer. If our sermons are going to reach the hearts and consciences of the people, we must be much in prayer to God, so that there may be power with the Word.

In the gospel of John we read that Jesus, at the grave of Lazarus, lifted up His eyes to heaven and said,

> *Father, I thank thee that thou hast heard me. And I knew that thou hearest me always: but because of the people which stand by I said it, that they may believe that thou hast sent me.* (John 11:41–42)

13

Notice that before He spoke to bring the dead back to life, He spoke to His Father. If our spiritually dead ones are to be raised, we must first be attuned to God. The reason we so often fail in moving our fellowmen is that we try to win them without first receiving the power to do so from God. Jesus was in communion with His Father; therefore, He could be assured that His prayers were heard.

We read again, in the twelfth chapter of John, that Jesus prayed to the Father. I think this is one of the saddest chapters in the whole Bible. He was about to leave the Jewish nation and make atonement for the sin of the world. Hear what He said: *"Now is my soul troubled; and what shall I say? Father, save me from this hour: but for this cause came I unto this hour"* (John 12:27). He was almost under the shadow of the cross; the iniquities of mankind were about to be laid upon Him. One of His twelve disciples was going to deny Him and swear he never knew Him. Another was about to sell Him for thirty pieces of silver. All were going to forsake Him and flee. His soul was exceedingly sorrowful, and He prayed. When His soul was troubled, God spoke to Him. In answer to His cry, *"Father, glorify thy name,"* He heard a voice coming down from heaven, *"I have both glorified it, and will glorify it again"* (John 12:28).

Another memorable prayer of our Lord was in the Garden of Gethsemane: *"He was withdrawn from them about a stone's cast, and kneeled down, and prayed"* (Luke 22:41). While He prayed, an angel appeared to strengthen Him (v. 43).

I would draw your attention to the recorded fact that four times the answer came right down from heaven while the Savior prayed to God. The first time was at His baptism, when the heavens were opened and the Spirit descended upon Him in answer to His prayer. Again, on the Mount of Transfiguration, God appeared and spoke to Him. Then, when the Greeks came desiring to see Him, the voice of God was heard responding to His call; and again, when He cried to the Father in the midst of His agony, a direct response was given. These things are recorded, I am sure, so that we may be encouraged to pray.

We read that His disciples came to Him and said, *"Lord, teach us to pray"* (Luke 11:1). It is not recorded that He taught them how to preach. I have often said that I would rather know how to pray like Daniel than preach like Gabriel. If you get real love into your soul, so that the grace of God may come down in answer to prayer, you will have no trouble reaching the people. It is not by eloquent sermons that perishing souls are going to be reached; we need the power of God in order for the blessing to come down.

The prayer our Lord taught His disciples (see Matthew 6:9–13) is commonly called the Lord's Prayer, but I prefer to call it the Disciples' Prayer. I think that the Lord's prayer, more properly, is the one found in the seventeenth chapter of John. That is the longest prayer on record that Jesus made. You can read it slowly and carefully in about four or five minutes. I think we may learn a lesson here. Our Master's prayers were short when offered in public; when He was alone with God that was a different thing, and He could spend the whole night in communion with His Father.

My experience is that those who pray a lot in their prayer closets generally make short prayers in public. Long prayers are too often not prayers at all, and they weary others. How short the publican's prayer was! *"God be merciful to me a sinner"* (Luke 18:13). The cry of the Syrophenician woman was shorter still: *"Lord, help me"* (Matt. 15:25). She went right to the mark, and she got what she wanted. The prayer of the thief on the cross was a short one: *"Lord, remember me when thou comest into thy kingdom"* (Luke 23:42). Peter's prayer was, *"Lord, save me"* (Matt. 14:30). So, if you go through the Scriptures, you will find that the prayers that brought immediate answers were generally brief. Let our prayers be to the point, just telling God what we need.

In the prayer of our Lord, in John 17, we find that He made seven requests—one for Himself, four for His disciples around Him, and two for the disciples of succeeding ages. Six times in that one prayer He repeated that God had sent Him. The world looked upon Him as an imposter, and He wanted them to know that He was heaven-sent. He spoke of the world nine times and made mention of His disciples and those who believe on Him fifty times.

Christ's last prayer on the cross was a short one: *"Father, forgive them; for they know not what they do"* (Luke 23:34). I believe that prayer was answered. We find that right there in front of the cross, a Roman centurion was converted. (See Luke 23:47.) It was probably in answer to the Savior's prayer. The conversion of the thief (see Luke 23:39–43), I believe, was in answer to that same prayer of our blessed Lord. Saul of Tarsus may have heard it that day, and the words may have followed him as he traveled to Damascus; thus, when the Lord spoke to him on the way, he may have recognized the voice. (See Acts 9:3–6.) One thing we do know: on the Day of Pentecost some of the enemies of the Lord were converted. (See Acts 2:22–23, 37–41.) Surely that was in answer to the prayer, *"Father, forgive them!"*

Hence, we see that prayer holds a high place among the exercises of a spiritual life. All God's people have been praying people. Look, for instance, at Richard Baxter. He stained his study walls with praying breath, and after he was anointed with the unction of the Holy Spirit, he sent a river of living water over Kidderminster and converted hundreds. Martin Luther and his companions were men of such mighty pleading with God that they broke the spell of ages and laid nations subdued at the foot of the cross. John Knox grasped all of Scotland in his strong arms of faith; his prayers terrified tyrants. George Whitefield, after much holy, faithful prayer-closet pleading, went to the devil's fair and took more than a thousand souls out of the paw of the lion in one day. See a praying Wesley turn more than ten thousand souls to the Lord! Look at the praying Finney, whose prayers, faith, sermons, and writings have shaken all of America and have sent a wave of blessing through the churches in both America and England.

Dr. Guthrie said this about prayer and its necessity:

The first true sign of spiritual life, prayer, is also the means of maintaining it. Man can as well live physically without breathing, as spiritually without praying. There is a class of animals—the cetaceous,[1] neither fish nor seafowl—that inhabit the deep. It is their home, they never leave it for the shore; yet, though swimming beneath its waves, and sounding its darkest depths, they have ever and anon to rise to the surface that they may breathe the air. Without that, these monarchs of the deep could not exist in the dense element in which they *"live, and move, and have* [their] *being"* (Acts 17:28).

And something like what is imposed on them by a physical necessity, the Christian has to do by a spiritual one. It is by ever and anon ascending up to God, by rising through prayer into a loftier, purer region for supplies of divine grace, that he maintains his spiritual life. Prevent these animals from rising to the surface, and they die for want of breath; prevent the Christian from rising to God, and he dies for want of prayer. *"Give me children,"* cried Rachel, *"or else I die"* (Gen. 30:1). "Let me breathe," says a man gasping, "or else I die." "Let me pray," says the Christian, "or else I die."

"Since I began," said Dr. Payson when a student, "to beg God's blessing on my studies, I

---

[1] Cetaceous: the Cetacea order of animals, which includes whales, dolphins, porpoises, and similar mammals.

have done more in one week than in the whole year before." Luther, when most pressed with work, said, "I have so much to do that I cannot get on without three hours a day praying." Not only do theologians think and speak highly of prayer, but men of all ranks and positions in life have also felt the same. If the hour for marching was six o'clock, General Havelock rose at four, rather than lose the precious privilege of communion with God before setting out. Sir Matthew Hale, an English jurist, said, "If I omit praying and reading God's Word in the morning, nothing goes well all day."

"A great part of my time," said Robert Murray McCheyne, "is spent in getting my heart in tune for prayer. It is the link that connects earth with heaven."

A comprehensive view of the subject will show that there are nine elements that are essential to true prayer. The first is *adoration*; we cannot meet God up close from the start. We must approach Him as One far beyond our reach or sight. The next is *confession*; sin must be put out of the way. We cannot have any communion with God while there is any transgression between us. If there is some wrong that you have done against a person, you cannot expect that person's favor until you go to him and confess the fault.

Restitution is another essential element; we have to make good the wrong, wherever possible. *Thanksgiving* is the next; we must be thankful for what God has done for us already. Then comes *forgiveness*, and next *unity*. Then, for the kind of prayer these things produce, there must be *faith*.

Influenced by these seven elements, we will be ready to offer direct *petition.* We hear a good deal of praying that is just exhorting, and often if you did not see the eyes closed of the one praying, you would suppose he was preaching. Also, much that is called prayer is simply finding fault. We need more petition in our prayers.

After all these, there must come *submission.* While praying, we must be ready to accept the will of God. We will consider these nine elements in detail, closing our inquiries by giving incidents illustrative of the certainty of our receiving, under such conditions, answers to prayer.

The Trinity

Thou dear and great mysterious Three,
    Forever be adored,
For all the endless grace we see
    In our Redeemer stored.

The Father's ancient grace we sing,
    That chose us in our Head;
Ordaining Christ, our God and King,
    To suffer in our stead.

The sacred Son, in equal strains,
    With reverence we address,
For all His grace, and dying pains,
    And splendid righteousness.

With tuneful tongue the Holy Ghost
    For His great work we praise,
Whose power inspires the blood-bought host
    Their grateful voice to raise.

Thus the Eternal Three in One
    We join to praise, for grace
And endless glory through the Son,
    As shining from His face.

—*Author Unknown*

CHAPTER 2

Adoration

Adoration has been defined as the act of rendering divine honor, including in it reverence, esteem, and love. It literally means, "to apply the hand to the mouth, to kiss the hand"; in Eastern countries this is one of the great marks of respect and submission. The importance of coming before God in this spirit is great; therefore, it is so often impressed upon us in the Word of God.

The Reverend Newman Hall, in his work on the Lord's Prayer, said,

> Man's worship, apart from revelation, has been uniformly characterized by selfishness. We come to God either to thank Him for benefits already received, or to implore still further benefits: food, raiment, health, safety, comfort. Like Jacob at Bethel, we are disposed to make the worship we render to God correlative with *"bread to eat, and raiment to put on"* (Gen. 28:20).
>
> This style of petition, in which self generally precedes and predominates, if it

does not altogether absorb our supplications, is not only seen in the votaries of false systems, but in the majority of the prayers of professed Christians. Our prayers are like the Parthian horsemen, who ride one way while they look another; we seem to go toward God, but, indeed, reflect upon ourselves. And this may be the reason why many times our prayers are sent forth, like the raven out of Noah's ark, and never return. But when we make the glory of God the chief end of our devotion, they go forth like the dove and return to us again with an olive branch.

Let me refer you to a passage in the prophecies of Daniel. He was one of the men who knew how to pray. His prayer brought the blessing of heaven upon himself and upon his people. He said,

> *I set my face unto the Lord God, to seek by prayer and supplications, with fasting, and sackcloth, and ashes: and I prayed unto the LORD my God, and made my confession, and said, O Lord, the great and dreadful God, keeping the covenant and mercy to them that love him, and to them that keep his commandments.* (Dan. 9:3–4)

The thought I want to call special attention to is conveyed in the words, *"O Lord, the great and dreadful God."* Daniel took his rightful place before God—in the dust—and he put God in His rightful place.

It was when Abraham was on his face, prostrate before God, that God spoke to him. (See

24

Genesis 17:3.) Holiness belongs to God; sinfulness belongs to us.

Brooks, that grand old Puritan writer, said,

> A person of real holiness is much affected and taken up in the admiration of the holiness of God. Unholy persons may be somewhat affected and taken with the other excellencies of God; it is only holy souls that are taken and affected with His holiness. The more holy any are, the more deeply are they affected by this. To the holy angels, the holiness of God is the sparkling diamond in the ring of glory. But unholy persons are affected and taken with anything rather than with this.
>
> Nothing strikes the sinner into such a dejection as a discourse on the holiness of God; it is as the handwriting on the wall; nothing makes the head and heart of a sinner to ache like a sermon upon the Holy One; nothing galls and gripes, nothing stings and terrifies unsanctified ones, like a lively setting forth of the holiness of God. But to holy souls there are no discourses that suit and satisfy them more, that delight and content them more, that please and profit them more, than those that most fully and powerfully discover God to be glorious in holiness.

So, in coming before God, we must adore and reverence His name. The same thing is brought out in the book of Isaiah:

In the year that king Uzziah died I saw also the Lord sitting upon a throne, high and

> *lifted up, and his train filled the temple.*
> *Above it stood the seraphims: each one had*
> *six wings; with twain he covered his face,*
> *and with twain he covered his feet, and*
> *with twain he did fly. And one cried unto*
> *another, and said, Holy, holy, holy, is the*
> *LORD of hosts: the whole earth is full of his*
> *glory.* (Isa. 6:1–3)

When we see the holiness of God, we will adore and magnify Him. Moses had to learn the same lesson. God told him to take off his shoes, for the place where he stood was holy ground (Exod. 3:5). Men who speak about their holiness and try to claim that they are holy make light of the holiness of God. It is His holiness that we need to think and speak about; when we do that, we will be prostrate in the dust.

You remember also how it was with Peter. When Christ made Himself known to him, he said, *"Depart from me; for I am a sinful man, O Lord"* (Luke 5:8). A sight of God is enough to show us how holy He is, and how unholy we are.

We find that Job, too, had to be taught the same lesson: *"Then Job answered the LORD, and said, Behold, I am vile; what shall I answer thee? I will lay mine hand upon my mouth"* (Job 40:3–4). As you hear Job having discussions with his friends, you would think he was one of the holiest men who ever lived. He was *"eyes to the blind, and feet...to the lame"* (Job 29:15); he fed the hungry and clothed the naked. What a wonderfully good man he was! It was all I, I, I. At last God said to him, *"'Gird up now thy loins like a man'* (Job 38:3), and I will put a few questions to you." The moment that God revealed Himself, Job changed his speech. He saw his own vileness and God's purity. He cried out, *"I have heard of thee by the hearing of the ear: but now mine eye seeth thee. Wherefore I abhor myself, and repent in dust and ashes"* (Job 42:5–6).

The same thing is seen in the cases of those who came to our Lord in the days that He walked the earth; those who came in the right way, seeking and obtaining the blessing, manifested a lively sense of His infinite superiority to themselves. The centurion, of whom we read in Matthew, said, *"Lord, I am not worthy that thou shouldest come under my roof"* (Matt. 8:8). Jairus worshipped Him as he presented his request. (See Mark 5:22–23.) The leper, in the gospel of Mark, came *"kneeling down to him"* (Mark 1:40). The Syrophenician woman *"came and fell at his feet"* (Mark 7:25). Upon *"seeing Jesus,"* the man full of leprosy *"fell on his face"* (Luke 5:12). So, too, the beloved disciple, speaking of the feeling the disciples had when they were abiding with their Lord, said, *"We beheld his glory, the glory as of the only begotten of the Father, full of grace and truth"* (John 1:14). However intimate their companionship and tender their love, they reverenced as much as they communed and adored as much as they loved.

We may say of every act of prayer what George Herbert, an English clergyman, said of public worship:

When once thy foot enters the church, be bare;
God is more than thou; for thou art there
Only by His permission. Then beware,

And make thyself all reverence and fear.
Kneeling ne'er spoiled silk stocking; quit thy state.
All equal are within the church's gate.

The wise man, Solomon, said,

Keep thy foot when thou goest to the house of God, and be more ready to hear, than to give the sacrifice of fools: for they consider not that they do evil. Be not rash with thy mouth, and let not thine heart be hasty to utter any thing before God: for God is in heaven, and thou upon earth: therefore let thy words be few. (Eccl. 5:1–2)

If we are struggling to live a higher life and to know something of God's holiness and purity, what we need is to be brought into contact with Him, that He may reveal Himself. Then we will take our place before Him as those men of old were constrained to do. We will hallow His name, as the Master taught His disciples when He said, *"Hallowed be thy name"* (Matt. 6:9). When I think of the irreverence of the present time, it seems to me that we are living in evil days.

Let us, as Christians, when we draw near to God in prayer, give Him His rightful place. *"Let us have grace, whereby we may serve God acceptably with reverence and godly fear: for our God is a consuming fire"* (Heb. 12:28–29).

Confession

No, not despairingly
    Come I to Thee;
No, not distrustingly
    Bend I the knee;
Sin hath gone over me,
Yet is this still my plea,
    Jesus hath died.

Ah, mine iniquity
    Crimson has been;
Infinite, infinite,
    Sin upon sin;
Sin of not loving Thee,
Sin of not trusting Thee.
    Infinite sin.

Lord, I confess to Thee
    Sadly my sin;
All I am, tell I Thee,
    All I have been.
Purge Thou my sin away,
Wash Thou my soul this day;
    Lord, make me clean!

—*Dr. H. Bonar*

CHAPTER 3

Confession

A nother element in true prayer is confession. I do not want Christian friends to think that I am talking to the unsaved. I think that, as Christians, we have many sins to confess.

If you go back to the Scripture records, you will find that the men who lived nearest to God and had the most power with Him were those who confessed their sins and failures. Daniel, as we have seen, confessed his sins and those of his people. (See Daniel 9:20.) Yet there is nothing recorded against Daniel. He was one of the best men on the face of the earth, yet his confession of sin was one of the deepest and most humble on record. Brooks, referring to Daniel's confession, said,

> In these words (Dan. 9:5–6), you have seven circumstances that Daniel uses in confessing his and the people's sins, and all to heighten and aggravate them. First, *"We have sinned"*; secondly, *"We have committed iniquity"*; thirdly, *"We have done wickedly"*; fourthly, *"We have rebelled against thee"*; fifthly, *"We have departed from thy precepts"*;

sixthly, *"We have not hearkened unto thy servants"*; seventhly, *"Nor our princes, nor all the people of the land."* These seven aggravations which Daniel reckons up in his confession are worthy of our most serious consideration.

Job was no doubt a holy man, a mighty prince, yet he had to fall in the dust and confess his sins. You will find the necessity of confession all through the Bible. When Isaiah saw the purity and holiness of God, he beheld himself in his true state and exclaimed, *"Woe is me! for I am undone; because I am a man of unclean lips"* (Isa. 6:5).

I firmly believe that the church of God will have to confess her own sins before there can be any great work of grace. There must be a deeper work among God's believing people. I sometimes think it is about time to give up preaching to the ungodly and preach to those who profess to be Christians. If we had a higher standard of life in the church of God, there would be thousands more flocking into the kingdom. It was so in the past; when God's believing children turned away from their sins and their idols, the fear of God fell upon the people around them. Look at the history of Israel, and you will find that when they put away their strange gods, God visited the nation, and there came a mighty work of grace.

What we want in these days is a true, deep revival in the church of God. I have little sympathy with the idea that God is going to reach the masses by a cold, formal church. *"The time is come that judgment must begin at the house of God"* (1 Pet. 4:17)—with us.

Notice that when Daniel got that wonderful answer to prayer recorded in the ninth chapter, he was confessing his sin. That is one of the best chapters on prayer in the whole Bible. We read,

And whiles I was speaking, and praying, and confessing my sin and the sin of my people Israel, and presenting my supplication before the LORD my God for the holy mountain of my God; yea, whiles I was speaking in prayer, even the man Gabriel, whom I had seen in the vision at the beginning, being caused to fly swiftly, touched me about the time of the evening oblation. And he informed me, and talked with me, and said, O Daniel, I am now come forth to give thee skill and understanding.

(Dan. 9:20–22)

So, too, when Job was confessing his sin, God turned his captivity and heard his prayer. God will hear our prayer and turn our captivity when we take our true place before Him and confess and forsake our transgressions. It was when Isaiah cried out before the Lord, *"I am undone"* (Isa. 6:5), that the blessing came; the live coal was taken from the altar and put upon his lips, and he went out to write one of the most wonderful books the world has ever seen. What a blessing it has been to the church!

It was when David said, *"I have sinned"* (2 Sam. 12:13), that God dealt in mercy with him. He confessed his sin to God:

I acknowledged my sin unto thee, and mine iniquity have I not hid. I said, I will confess

33

my transgressions unto the LORD; and thou forgavest the iniquity of my sin. (Ps. 32:5)

Notice how David made a very similar confession to that of the prodigal in the fifteenth chapter of Luke. These are the words of the prodigal son:

And the son said unto him, Father, I have sinned against heaven, and in thy sight, and am no more worthy to be called thy son. (Luke 15:21)

David's confession went as follows:

For I acknowledge my transgressions: and my sin is ever before me. Against thee, thee only, have I sinned, and done this evil in thy sight. (Ps. 51:3–4)

There is no difference between the king and the beggar when the Spirit of God comes into the heart and convicts of sin.

Richard Sibbes, a Puritan preacher, quaintly said of confession,

This is the way to give glory to God: when we have laid open our souls to God, and laid as much against ourselves as the devil could do that way, for let us think what the devil would lay to our charge at the hour of death and the day of judgment. He would lay hard to our charge this and that—let us accuse ourselves as he would, and as he will ere long. The more we accuse and judge ourselves, and set up a tribunal in our hearts, certainly there will follow an incredible ease. Jonah was cast into the sea, and there was an ease in the ship; Achan was stoned, and the plague was stayed. Out with Jonah, out with Achan; and there will follow ease and quiet in the soul presently. Conscience will receive wonderful ease.

It must needs be so, for when God is honored, conscience is purified. God is honored by confession of sin every way. It honors His omniscience that He is all-seeing, that He sees our sins and searches our hearts—our secrets are not hid from Him. It honors His power. What makes us confess our sins, but that we are afraid of His power, lest He should execute it? And what makes us confess our sins, but that we know there is mercy with Him that He may be feared, and that there is pardon for sin? We would not confess our sins else. With men it is, Confess and have execution; but with God it is, Confess and have mercy. It is His own protestation. We should never lay open our sins but for mercy. So it honors God; and when He is honored, He honors the soul with inward peace and tranquillity.

Thomas Fuller, an English author and clergyman, said, "Man's owning his weakness is the only stock for God thereon to graft the grace of His assistance."

Confession implies humility, and humility, in God's sight, is of great price.

A farmer went with his son into a wheat field to see if it was ready for the harvest. "See, father," exclaimed the boy, "how straight these stems hold up their heads! They must be the best ones. Those that hang their heads down cannot be good for much, I am sure." The farmer plucked a stalk of each kind and said, "See here, foolish child! This stalk that stood so straight is light-headed and almost good for nothing, while this that hung its head so modestly is full of the most beautiful grain."

Outspokenness is necessary and powerful, both with God and man. We need to be honest and frank with ourselves. A soldier said in a revival meeting, "My fellow soldiers, I am not excited; I am *convinced*—that is all. I feel that I ought to be a Christian and that I ought to say so, to tell you so, and to ask you to come with me. Now, if there is a call for sinners seeking Christ to come forward, I for one shall go—not to make a show, for I have nothing but sin to show. I do not go because I want to—I would rather keep my seat—but going will be telling the truth. I ought to be a Christian, I want to be a Christian, and going forward for prayer is just telling the truth about it." More than twenty men went with him.

Speaking of Pharaoh's words, *"Entreat the LORD, that he may take away the frogs from me"* (Exod. 8:8), Charles Spurgeon said,

> A fatal flaw is manifest in that prayer. *It contains no confession of sin.* He says not, "I have rebelled against the Lord; entreat that I may find forgiveness!" Nothing of the kind; he loves sin as much as ever. A prayer without penitence is a prayer without acceptance. If no tear has fallen upon

it, it is withered. You must come to God as a sinner through a Savior, but by no other way. He who comes to God like the Pharisee, with, *"God, I thank thee, that I am not as other men are"* (Luke 18:11), never draws near to God at all; but he who cries, *"God be merciful to me a sinner"* (Luke 18:13), has come to God by the way which God has Himself appointed. There must be confession of sin before God, or our prayers are faulty.

If this confession of sin is deep among believers, it will be so among the ungodly also. I have never known it to fail. I am now anxious for God to revive His work in the hearts of His children so that we may see the exceeding sinfulness of sin. There are many Christian fathers and mothers who are anxious for the conversion of their children. I have had as many as fifty messages from parents come to me within a single week, wondering why their children are not saved and asking prayer for them. I venture to say that, as a rule, the fault lies at our own doors. (See Genesis 4:7.) There may be something in our lives that stands in the way. It may be there is some secret sin that keeps back the blessing. David lived in his awful sin for many months before Nathan made his appearance. Let us ask God to come into our hearts and make His power felt. If it is a right eye that causes us to sin, let us pluck it out; if it is a right hand, let us cut it off (see Matthew 5:29–30), so that we may have power with God and with man.

Why is it that so many of our children are wandering off into the barrooms and drifting away into unbelief—going down to a dishonored grave? There seems to be very little power in the Christianity of the present time. Many godly parents find that their children are going astray. Does it arise from some secret sin clinging around the parents' hearts? There is a passage of God's Word that is often quoted, but in ninety-nine cases out of a hundred, those who quote it stop at the wrong place. In the fifty-ninth chapter of Isaiah we read, *"Behold, the LORD'S hand is not shortened, that it cannot save; neither his ear heavy, that it cannot hear"* (v. 1). There they stop. Of course, God's hand is not shortened and His ear is not heavy, but we ought to read the next two verses:

> *But your iniquities have separated between you and your God, and your sins have hid his face from you, that he will not hear. For your hands are defiled with blood, and your fingers with iniquity; your lips have spoken lies, your tongue hath muttered perverseness.*　　　　　　　　(Isa. 59:2–3)

As Matthew Henry said, "It was owing to themselves—they stood in their own light, they shut their own door. God was coming toward them in the way of mercy, and they hindered Him. *'Your iniquities...and your sins have withholden good things from you'* (Jer. 5:25)."

Bear in mind that if we are regarding iniquity in our hearts or depending on an empty mouthing of our faith, we have no claim to expect that our prayers will be answered. (See Psalm 66:18.) There is not one solitary promise for us. I sometimes tremble when I hear people quote promises and say that God is bound to fulfill those promises to them, when all the time there is something in their own lives that they are not willing to give up. It is well for us to search our hearts and find out why it is that our prayers are not answered.

Let me quote a very solemn passage in Isaiah:

Hear the word of the LORD, ye rulers of Sodom; give ear unto the law of our God, ye people of Gomorrah. To what purpose is the multitude of your sacrifices unto me? saith the LORD: I am full of the burnt offerings of rams, and the fat of fed beasts; and I delight not in the blood of bullocks, or of lambs, or of he goats. When ye come to appear before me, who hath required this at your hand, to tread my courts? Bring no more vain oblations; incense is an abomination unto me; the new moons and sabbaths, the calling of assemblies, I cannot away with; it is iniquity, even the solemn meeting.
(Isa. 1:10–13)

"Even the solemn meeting"—think of that! If God does not get our heart services, He will have none of our outward services; they are an abomination to Him.

Your new moons and your appointed feasts my soul hateth: they are a trouble unto me; I am weary to bear them. And when ye spread forth your hands, I will hide mine eyes from you: yea, when ye make many prayers, I will not hear: your hands are full

*of blood. Wash you, make you clean; put
away the evil of your doings from before
mine eyes; cease to do evil; learn to do well;
seek judgment, relieve the oppressed, judge
the fatherless, plead for the widow. Come
now, and let us reason together, saith the
LORD: though your sins be as scarlet, they
shall be as white as snow; though they be
red like crimson, they shall be as wool.*

(Isa. 1:14–18)

Again we read in Proverbs, *"He that turneth
away his ear from hearing the law, even his prayer
shall be abomination"* (Prov. 28:9). Think of that!
It may shock some of us to think that our prayers are an abomination to God, yet if any are
living in known sin, this is what God's Word says
about them. If we are not willing to turn from sin
and obey God's law, we have no right to expect
that He will answer our prayers. Unconfessed sin
is unforgiven sin, and unforgiven sin is the darkest, foulest thing on this sin-cursed earth. You
cannot find a case in the Bible where a man has
been honest in dealing with sin and God has not
been honest with him and blessed him. The
prayer of the humble, contrite heart is a delight
to God. There is no sound that goes up from this
sin-cursed earth that is so sweet to His ear as
the prayer of the man who is walking uprightly.
Let me call attention to that prayer of David,
in which he said,

*Search me, O God, and know my heart: try
me, and know my thoughts: and see if there
be any wicked way in me, and lead me in
the way everlasting.* (Ps. 139:23–24)

I wish all my readers would commit these verses to memory. If we would all honestly make this prayer once every day, there would be a good deal of change in our lives. *"Search me"*—not my neighbor. It is so easy to pray for other people but so hard to get honest with ourselves. I am afraid that we who are busy in the Lord's work are very often in danger of neglecting our own vineyards. In this psalm, David got honest about himself. There is a difference between God searching me and my searching myself. I may search my heart and pronounce it all right, but when God searches me with His light, a lot of things come to light that perhaps I knew nothing about.

"Try me." David was tried when he fell by taking his eye off the God of his father Abraham. *"Know my thoughts."* God looks at the thoughts. Are our thoughts pure? Do we have in our hearts thoughts against God or against His people— against anyone in the world? If we have, we are not right in the sight of God. Oh, may God search us, all of us! I do not know any better prayer that we can make than this prayer of David. One of the most solemn truths in biblical history is that when holy men—better people than we are—were tested and tried, they were found to be as weak as water away from God.

Let us be sure that we are right with God. Isaac Ambrose, in his work "Self Trial," wrote the following pithy words:

Now and then propose we to our hearts these two questions: (1) "Heart, how dost thou?"—a few words, but a very serious question. You know this is the first question and the first salute that we use to one another—How do you do? I would to God we sometimes thus spoke to our hearts: "Heart, how dost thou? How is it with thee, for thy spiritual state?" (2) "Heart, what wilt thou do?" or, "Heart, what dost thou think will become of thee and me?"—as that dying Roman once said: "Poor, wretched, miserable soul, whither art thou and I going—and what will become of thee, when thou and I shall part?"

This very thing does Moses propose to Israel, though in other terms: *"O...that they would consider their latter end!"* (Deut. 32:29)—and, oh, that we would put this question constantly to our hearts, to consider and debate upon! *"Commune with your own heart"* (Ps. 4:4), said David; that is, debate the matter between you and your heart to the very utmost. Let your hearts be so put to it in communing with them that they may speak their very bottom. Commune—or hold a serious communication and clear intelligence and acquaintance—with your own heart.

The following is the confession of a theologian, sensible of his neglect, and especially of the difficulty of this duty:

I have lived forty years and somewhat more, and carried my heart in my bosom all this while, and yet my heart and I are as great strangers and as utterly unacquainted as if we had never come near one

another. No, I know not my heart; I have
forgotten my heart. Alas, alas, that I could
be grieved at the very heart, that my poor
heart and I have been so unacquainted!

We are fallen into an Athenian age,
spending our time in nothing more than
telling or hearing news. How go things
here? How there? How in one place? How
in another? But who is there that is in-
quisitive? How are things with my poor
heart? Weigh but in the balance of a serious consideration, what time we have
spent in this duty, and what time other-
wise; and for many scores and hundreds of
hours or days that we owe to our hearts in
this duty, can we write fifty? Or, where
there should have been fifty vessels full of
this duty, can we find twenty, or ten? Oh,
the days, months, years, we bestow upon
sin, vanity, the affairs of this world, while
we afford not a minute in converse with
our own hearts concerning their case!

If there is anything in our lives that is
wrong, let us ask God to show it to us. Have we
been selfish? Have we been more jealous of our
own reputation than of the honor of God? Elijah
thought he was very jealous for the honor of
God, but it turned out that it was his own honor
after all—self was really at the bottom of it.
One of the saddest things, I think, that
Christ had to meet with in His disciples was this
very thing; there was a constant struggle between them as to who should be the greatest,
instead of each one taking the humblest place
and being least in his own estimation.

We are told in proof of this, the following:

He came to Capernaum: and being in the house he asked them, What was it that ye disputed among yourselves by the way? But they held their peace: for by the way they had disputed among themselves, who should be the greatest. And he sat down, and called the twelve, and saith unto them, If any man desire to be first, the same shall be last of all, and servant of all. And he took a child, and set him in the midst of them: and when he had taken him in his arms, he said unto them, Whosoever shall receive one of such children in my name, receiveth me: and whosoever shall receive me, receiveth not me, but him that sent me.

(Mark 9:33–37)

Soon after that, a similar incident occurred:

James and John, the sons of Zebedee, come unto him, saying, Master, we would that thou shouldest do for us whatsoever we shall desire. And he said unto them, What would ye that I should do for you? They said unto him, Grant unto us that we may sit, one on thy right hand, and the other on thy left hand, in thy glory. But Jesus said unto them, Ye know not what ye ask: can ye drink of the cup that I drink of? and be baptized with the baptism that I am baptized with? And they said unto him, We can. And Jesus said unto them, Ye shall indeed drink of the cup that I drink of; and with the baptism that I am baptized withal shall ye be baptized: but to sit on my right hand and on my left hand is not mine to give; but it shall be given to them for whom it is prepared. And when the ten heard it, they began to be much displeased with James and John. But Jesus called them to him, and saith unto them, Ye know that they which are accounted to rule over the Gentiles exercise lordship over them; and their great ones exercise authority upon them. But so shall it not be among you: but whosoever will be great among you, shall be your minister: and whosoever of you will be the chiefest, shall be servant of all. For even the Son of man came not to be ministered unto, but to minister, and to give his life a ransom for many.

(Mark 10:35–45)

The latter words were spoken in the third year of His ministry. For three years the disciples had been with Him. They had listened to the words that fell from His lips, but they had failed to learn this lesson of humility. The most humiliating thing that happened among the Twelve occurred on the night of our Lord's betrayal, when Judas sold Him and Peter denied Him.

If there was any place where there should have been an absence of these thoughts about status and position, it was at the supper table. Yet, we find that when Christ instituted that blessed memorial there was a debate going on among His disciples about who would be the greatest. Think of that! Right before the cross, when the Master was *"exceeding sorrowful, even unto death"* (Matt. 26:38); when He was already tasting the bitterness of Calvary, and the horrors of that dark hour were gathering upon His soul!

I think if God searches us, we will find a lot of things in our lives to confess. If we are tried and tested by God's law, there will be many things that will have to be changed. I ask again: Are we selfish or jealous? Are we willing to hear of others being used by God more than we are? Are the Methodists willing to hear of a great revival of God's Word among the Baptists? Would it rejoice their souls to hear of such efforts being blessed? Are Baptists willing to hear of a reviving of God's work in the Methodist, Congregational, or other churches? If we are full of narrow party and sectarian feelings, there will be many things to be laid aside. Let us pray to God to search us, try us, and see if there is any evil way in us. If these holy and good men felt that they were faulty, should we not tremble and endeavor to find out if there is anything in our lives that God would have us get rid of?

Once again, let me call your attention to the prayer of David contained in the fifty-first Psalm. A friend of mine told me some years ago that he repeated this prayer as his own every week. I think it would be a good thing if we offered up these petitions frequently; let them go right up from our hearts. If we have been proud or irritable or lacking in patience, should we not at once confess it? Is it not time that we begin at home and get our lives straightened out? See how quickly the ungodly will then begin to inquire about the way of life! Let those of us who are parents set our own houses in order and be filled with Christ's Spirit; then it will not be long before our children will be asking what they must do to get the same Spirit.

I believe that today, by its lukewarmness and formality, the Christian church is making more infidels than all the books that infidels ever wrote. I do not fear infidel lectures half as much as the cold and dead formalism in the professing church at the present time. One prayer meeting like the one the disciples had on the Day of Pentecost would shake the whole infidel fraternity.

What we want is to get hold of God in prayer. We are not going to reach the masses by great sermons. We want to "move the arm that moves the world." To do that, we must be clean and right before God. As we read in 1 John,

> For if our heart condemn us, God is greater than our heart, and knoweth all things. Beloved, if our heart condemn us not, then have we confidence toward God. And whatsoever we ask, we receive of him, because we keep his commandments, and do those things that are pleasing in his sight.
>
> (1 John 3:20–22)

Perfect Cleansing

Who would be cleansed from every sin,
Must to God's holy altar bring
    The whole of life—its joys, its tears,
    Its hopes, its loves, its powers, its years,
The will, and every cherished thing!

Must make this sweeping sacrifice—
    Choose God, and dare reproach and shame,
    And boldly stand in storm or flame
For Him who paid redemption's price;
Then trust (not struggle to believe),
    And trusting wait, nor doubt, but pray
    That in His own good time He'll say,
"Thy faith hath saved thee; now receive."

His time is when the soul brings all,
    Is all upon His altar lain;
    When pride and self-conceit are slain,
And crucified with Christ, we fall
Helpless upon His word, and lie;
    When, faithful to His word, we feel
    The cleansing touch, the Spirit's seal,
And know that He does sanctify.

—*A. T. Allis*

CHAPTER 4

Restitution

A third element of successful prayer is restitution. If I have at any time taken what does not belong to me and am not willing to make restitution, my prayers will not go very far toward heaven. I find it amazing that I have never touched on this subject in my addresses without hearing of immediate results. A man once told me that I would not need to dwell on this point at a meeting that I was about to address because there would probably be no one present who would need to make restitution. However, I think if the Spirit of God searches our hearts, most of us will find a lot of things have to be done that we never thought of before.

After Zaccheus met with Christ, things looked altogether different. I venture to say that the idea of making restitution never entered his mind before. He probably thought that morning that he was a perfectly honest man. However, when the Lord came and spoke to him, he saw himself in an altogether different light. Notice how short his speech was. The only thing put on record that he said was this:

Behold, Lord, the half of my goods I give to the poor; and if I have taken any thing from any man by false accusation, I restore him fourfold. (Luke 19:8)

A short speech, but how the words have come ringing down through the ages!

By making that remark, he confessed his sin—that he had been dishonest. Besides that, he showed that he knew the requirements of the law of Moses. If a man had taken what did not belong to him, he was not only to return it, but to multiply it by four. I think that men in this dispensation ought to be as completely honest as men under the Law were. I am getting so tired and sick of mere sentimentalism, which does not straighten out a man's life. We may sing our hymns and psalms and offer prayers, but they will be an abomination to God unless we are willing to be thoroughly straightforward in our daily lives. Nothing will give Christianity such a hold on the world as to have God's believing people begin to act in this way. Zaccheus probably had more influence in Jericho after he made restitution than any other man there.

Charles Finney, in his lectures to professing Christians, said,

One reason for the requirement, *"Be not conformed to this world"* (Rom. 12:2), is the immense, salutary, and instantaneous influence it would have if everybody would do business on the principles of the Gospel. Turn the tables over, and let Christians do business one year on Gospel principles. It would shake the world! It would ring louder

than thunder. Let the ungodly see professing Christians in every transaction con-
sulting the good of the person they are
trading with—seeking not their own wealth,
but every man another's wealth (1 Cor.
10:24)—and living above the world—setting
no value on the world any further than it
would be the means of glorifying God. What
do you think would be the effect? It would
cover the world with confusion of face and
overwhelm them with conviction of sin.

Finney said that one grand mark of genuine
repentance is restitution:

The thief has not repented who keeps
the money he stole. He may have conviction, but no repentance. If he had repentance, he would go and give back the
money. If you have cheated anyone, and do
not restore what you have taken unjustly;
or if you have injured anyone, and do not
set about to undo the wrong you have
done, as far as in you lies, you have not
truly repented.

In Exodus we read, *"If a man shall steal an
ox, or a sheep, and kill it, or sell it; he shall restore
five oxen for an ox, and four sheep for a sheep"*
(Exod. 22:1). And again,

*If a man shall cause a field or vineyard to
be eaten, and shall put in his beast, and
shall feed in another man's field; of the best
of his own field, and of the best of his own
vineyard, shall he make restitution. If fire
break out, and catch in thorns, so that the*

*stacks of corn, or the standing corn, or the
field, be consumed therewith; he that kin-
dled the fire shall surely make restitution.*

(Exod. 22:5–6)

Or, turn to Leviticus, where the law of the
trespass offering is laid down, and the same point
is insisted on with equal clearness and force:

*If a soul sin, and commit a trespass against
the LORD, and lie unto his neighbour in that
which was delivered him to keep, or in fellowship, or in a thing taken away by vio-
lence, or hath deceived his neighbour; or
have found that which was lost, and lieth
concerning it, and sweareth falsely; in any
of all these that a man doeth, sinning
therein: then it shall be, because he hath
sinned, and is guilty, that he shall restore
that which he took violently away, or the
thing which he hath deceitfully gotten, or
that which was delivered him to keep, or
the lost thing which he found, or all that
about which he hath sworn falsely; he shall
even restore it in the principal, and shall
add the fifth part more thereto, and give it
unto him to whom it appertaineth, in the
day of his trespass offering.*   (Lev. 6:2–5)

The same thing is repeated in Numbers,
where we read,

*And the LORD spake unto Moses, saying,
Speak unto the children of Israel, When a
man or woman shall commit any sin that
men commit, to do a trespass against the
LORD, and that person be guilty; then they*

*shall confess their sin which they have
done: and he shall recompense his trespass
with the principal thereof, and add unto it
the fifth part thereof, and give it unto him
against whom he hath trespassed. But if
the man have no kinsman to recompense
the trespass unto, let the trespass be rec-
ompensed unto the LORD, even to the priest;
beside the ram of the atonement, whereby
an atonement shall be made for him.*

(Num. 5:5–8)

These were the laws that God laid down for
His people, and I believe their principle is as
binding today as it was then. If we have taken
anything from any man, if we have in any way
defrauded a man, let us not only confess it, but
also do all we can to make restitution. If we have
misrepresented anyone—if we have started some
slander or some false report about him—let us
do all in our power to undo the wrong.

It is in reference to a practical righteousness
such as this that we find written in Isaiah,

*Behold, ye fast for strife and debate, and to
smite with the fist of wickedness: ye shall
not fast as ye do this day, to make your
voice to be heard on high. Is it such a fast
that I have chosen? a day for a man to afflict his soul? is it to bow down his head as
a bulrush, and to spread sackcloth and
ashes under him? wilt thou call this a fast,
and an acceptable day to the LORD? Is not
this the fast that I have chosen? to loose the
bands of wickedness, to undo the heavy
burdens, and to let the oppressed go free,*

and that ye break every yoke? Is it not to deal thy bread to the hungry, and that thou bring the poor that are cast out to thy house? when thou seest the naked, that thou cover him; and that thou hide not thyself from thine own flesh? Then shall thy light break forth as the morning, and thine health shall spring forth speedily: and thy righteousness shall go before thee; the glory of the LORD shall be thy rereward [or, rear guard]. Then shalt thou call, and the LORD shall answer; thou shalt cry, and he shall say, Here I am.

(Isa. 58:4–9)

Trapp, in his comment about Zaccheus, said,

Sultan Selymus could tell his counselor Pyrrhus, who persuaded him to bestow the great wealth he had taken from the Persian merchants upon some notable hospital for relief of the poor, that God hates robbery for burnt offering. The dying Turk commanded it rather to be restored to the right owners, which was done accordingly, to the great shame of many Christians, who mind [obey] nothing less than restitution. When Henry III of England had sent the Friar Minors a load of frieze[2] to clothe them, they returned the same with this message: "That he ought not to give alms of what he had rent from the poor; neither would they accept of that abominable gift."

Master Latimer said, "If ye make no restitution of goods detained, ye shall cough in hell, and the devils shall laugh at

---

[2] Frieze: a heavy, coarse wool cloth.

56

you." Henry VII, in his last will and testament, after the disposition of his soul and body, devised and willed restitution should be made of all such moneys as had unjustly been levied by his officers. Queen Mary restored again all ecclesiastical livings assumed to the crown, saying that she set more by the salvation of her own soul than she did by ten kingdoms. [An edict] came also from the Pope, at the same time, that others should do likewise, but none did. Latimer tells us that the first day he preached about restitution, one came and gave him £20 to restore; the next day another brought him £30; another time someone gave him £200.

Mr. Bradford, hearing Latimer on that subject, was struck in the heart for one dash of the pen which he had made without the knowledge of his master and could never be quiet till, by the advice of Mr. Latimer, restitution was made, for which he did willingly forego all the private and certain patrimony which he had on earth.

"I, myself," said Mr. Barroughs, "knew one man who had wronged another but of five shillings, and fifty years after could not be quiet till he had restored it."

If there is true repentance, it will bring forth fruit. If we have done wrong to someone, we should never ask God to forgive us until we are willing to make restitution. If I have done any man a great injustice and can make it good, I need not ask God to forgive me until I am willing to do so. Suppose I have taken something that does not belong to me. I cannot expect forgiveness until I make restitution.

I remember preaching in an Eastern city, and a fine-looking man came up to me at the close. He was in great distress of mind. "The fact is," he said, "I am a defaulter. I have taken money that belonged to my employers. How can I become a Christian without restoring it?"

"Have you got the money?" He told me he did not have it all. He had taken about fifteen hundred dollars, and he still had about nine hundred.

He said, "Couldn't I take that money and go into business and make enough to pay them back?" I told him that this was a delusion of Satan, that he could not expect to prosper on stolen money, that he should restore all he had and go and ask his employers to have mercy upon him and forgive him. "But they will put me in prison," he said. "Can't you give me any help?"

"No, you must restore the money before you can expect to get any help from God."

"It is pretty hard," he said.

"Yes, it is hard, but the great mistake was doing the wrong in the first place." His burden became so heavy that it was, in fact, unbearable. He handed me the money—nine hundred fifty dollars and some cents—and asked me to take it back to his employers. I told them the story and said that he wanted mercy from them, not justice.

The tears trickled down the cheeks of those two men, and they said, "Forgive him! Yes, we will be glad to forgive him." I went downstairs and brought him up. After he had confessed his guilt and been forgiven, we all fell down on our knees and had a blessed prayer meeting. God met us and blessed us there.

Another friend of mine who had come to Christ was trying to consecrate himself and his wealth to God. He had formerly had transactions with the government and had taken advantage of them. This thing came to memory, and his conscience troubled him. He had a terrible struggle; his conscience kept rising up and smiting him. At last he wrote a check for fifteen hundred dollars and sent it to the treasury of the government. He told me he received such a blessing after he had done it. That is bringing forth *"fruits meet for repentance"* (Matt. 3:8). I believe many men are crying to God for light, and they are not getting it because they are not honest.

A man came to one of our meetings where this subject was touched on. The memory of a dishonest transaction flashed into his mind. He saw at once how it was that his prayers were not answered, but *"returned into* [his] *own bosom"* (Ps. 35:13). He left the meeting, took a train, and went to a distant city, where he had defrauded his employer years before. He went straight to this man, confessed the wrong, and offered to make restitution. Then he remembered another transaction in which he had failed to meet the just demands upon him; he at once made arrangements to have a large amount repaid. He came back to the place where we were holding the meetings, and God blessed him wonderfully in his own soul. I have not met a man for a long time who seemed to have received such a blessing.

Some years ago, in the north of England, a woman came to one of the meetings and appeared to be very anxious about her soul. She did not seem to be able to get peace for some time. The truth was, she was covering up one thing that she was not willing to confess. At last the burden was too great, and she said to a worker, "I never go down on my knees to pray, without a few bottles of wine coming up before my mind." It appeared that, years before, when she was a housekeeper, she had taken some bottles of wine belonging to her employer.

The worker asked, "Why do you not make restitution?" The woman replied that the man was dead, and besides, she did not know how much the wine was worth. "Are there any heirs living to whom you can make restitution?" She said there was a son living at some distance, but she thought it would be a very humiliating thing, so she held back for some time.

At last, she felt as if she must have a clear conscience at any cost, so she took the train and went to the place where the son of her previous employer resided. She took five pounds with her; she did not know exactly what the wine was worth, but that would cover it at any rate. The man said he did not want the money, but she replied, "I do not want it either; it has burnt a hole in my pocket long enough." He agreed to take half of it and give it to some charitable organization. Then she came back, and I think she was one of the happiest mortals I have ever met with. She said she could not tell whether she was in the body or out of it—such a blessing had come to her soul. (See 2 Corinthians 12:2–4.)

It may be that there is something in our lives that needs straightening out, something that happened perhaps decades ago and that has been forgotten until the Spirit of God brought it to our remembrance. If we are not willing to make restitution, we cannot expect God to give us a great blessing. Perhaps that is the reason so many of our prayers are not answered.

The Praise of God

Speak, lips of mine!
   And tell abroad
   The praises of my God.
Speak, stammering tongue!
   In gladdest tone,
   Make His high praises known.

Speak, sea and earth!
   Heaven's utmost star,
   Speak from your realms afar!
Take up the note,
   And send it round
   Creation's farthest bound.

Speak, heaven of heavens!
   Wherein our God
   Has made His bright abode.
Speak, angels, speak!
   In songs proclaim
   His everlasting name.

Speak, son of dust!
   Thy flesh He took
   And heaven for thee forsook.
Speak, child of death!
   Thy death He died,
   Bless thou the Crucified.

—*Dr. Bonar*

CHAPTER 5

Thanksgiving

The next element of prayer I want to discuss is thanksgiving. We ought to be more thankful for what we receive from God. Perhaps some of you who are mothers have a child in your family who is constantly complaining, never thankful. You know that there is not much pleasure in doing anything for a child like that. If you meet a beggar who is always grumbling and never seems to be thankful for what you give, you very soon shut the door in his face altogether. Ingratitude is about the hardest thing we have to deal with. Shakespeare wrote,

> Blow, blow, thou winter wind,
> Thou art not so unkind
>   As man's ingratitude;
> Thy tooth is not so keen,
> Because thou art not seen,
>   Although thy breath be rude.

We cannot speak too plainly of this evil, which so demeans those who are guilty of it. Even in Christians there is too much ingratitude! Here we are, getting blessings from God day after day, yet how little praise and thanksgiving there is in the church of God!

Gurnall, in his *Christian Armor,* referring to the words, *"In every thing give thanks"* (1 Thess. 5:18), said,

> *"Praise is comely for the upright"* (Ps. 33:1). "An unthankful saint" carries a contradiction with it. Evil and Unthankful are twins that live and die together; if anyone ceases to be evil, he begins to be thankful. Thanksgiving is that which God expects at your hands; He made you for this end. When the vote passed in heaven for your being—yes, happy being in Christ!—it was upon this account, that you should be a name and a praise to Him on earth in time, and in heaven to eternity. Should God miss this, He would fail of one main part of His design. What prompts Him to bestow every mercy, but to afford you matter to compose a song for His praise? *"They are my people, children that will not lie: so he was their Saviour"* (Isa. 63:8).
>
> He looks for fair dealing at your hands. Whom may a father trust with his reputation, if not his child? Where can a prince expect honor, if not among his favorites? Your state is such that the least mercy you have is more than all the world besides. Thou, Christian, and thy few brethren, divide heaven and earth among you! What has God that He withholds from you? Sun, moon, and stars are set up to give you light; sea and land have their treasures for your use; others are encroachers upon them; you are the rightful heirs to them; they groan that any others should be served by them.

The angels, bad and good, minister unto you; the evil, against their will, are forced like scullions[3] when they tempt you, to scour and brighten your graces, and make way for your greater comforts; the good angels are servants to your heavenly Father, and disdain not to carry you in their arms.

Your God withholds not Himself from you; He is your portion—Father, Husband, Friend. God is His own happiness, and admits you to enjoy Him. Oh, what honor is this, for the subject to drink from his prince's cup! *"Thou shalt make them drink of the river of thy pleasures"* (Ps. 36:8). And all this is not the purchase of your sweat and blood; the feast is paid for by Another, only He expects your thanks to the Founder. No sin offering is imposed under the Gospel; thank offerings are all He looks for.

Charnock, in discoursing on spiritual worship, said,

The praise of God is the choicest sacrifice and worship, under a dispensation of redeeming grace. This is the prime and eternal part of worship under the Gospel. The psalmist, speaking of the Gospel times, spurs on to this kind of worship: *"Sing unto the LORD a new song....Let the children of Zion be joyful in their King....Let the saints be joyful in glory: let them sing aloud upon their beds. Let the high praises of God be in their mouth"* (Ps. 149:1–2, 5–6). He begins

---

[3] Scullions: servants that do the hard, unpleasant work in the kitchen.

and ends [Psalm 149] with *Praise ye the Lord!*

That cannot be a spiritual and evangelical worship that has nothing of the praise of God in the heart. The consideration of God's adorable perfections discovered in the Gospel will make us come to Him with more seriousness, beg blessings of Him with more confidence, fly to Him with a winged faith and love, and more spiritually glorify Him in our attendance upon Him.

There is a great deal more said in the Bible about praise than prayer, yet how few praise meetings there are! David, in his psalms, always mixed praise with prayer. Solomon prevailed much with God in prayer at the dedication of the temple, but it was the voice of praise that brought down the glory that filled the house, for we read,

> *And it came to pass, when the priests were come out of the holy place: (for all the priests that were present were sanctified, and did not then wait by course: also the Levites which were the singers, all of them of Asaph, of Heman, of Jeduthun, with their sons and their brethren, being arrayed in white linen, having cymbals and psalteries and harps, stood at the east end of the altar, and with them an hundred and twenty priests sounding with trumpets:) it came even to pass, as the trumpeters and singers were as one, to make one sound to be heard in praising and thanking the LORD; and*

when they lifted up their voice with the trumpets and cymbals and instruments of music, and praised the LORD, saying, For he is good; for his mercy endureth for ever: that then the house was filled with a cloud, even the house of the LORD; so that the priests could not stand to minister by reason of the cloud: for the glory of the LORD had filled the house of God. (2 Chron. 5:11–14)

We read, too, of Jehoshaphat, that he gained the victory over the hosts of Ammon and Moab through praise, which was excited by faith and thankfulness to God:

And they rose early in the morning, and went forth into the wilderness of Tekoa: and as they went forth, Jehoshaphat stood and said, Hear me, O Judah, and ye inhabitants of Jerusalem; Believe in the LORD your God, so shall ye be established; believe his prophets, so shall ye prosper. And when he had consulted with the people, he appointed singers unto the LORD, and that should praise the beauty of holiness, as they went out before the army, and to say, Praise the LORD; for his mercy endureth for ever. And when they began to sing and to praise, the LORD set ambushments against the children of Ammon, Moab, and mount Seir, which were come against Judah; and they were smitten. (2 Chron. 20:20–22)

It is said that in a time of great despondency among the first settlers in New England, it was proposed in one of their public assemblies to proclaim a fast. An old farmer arose. He spoke of their provoking heaven with their complaints. He reviewed their measures, showed that they had much to be thankful for, and moved that instead of appointing a day of fasting, they should appoint a day of thanksgiving. This was done, and the custom has been continued ever since.

However great our difficulties, however deep our sorrows, there is room for thankfulness. Thomas Adams said,

> Lay up in the ark of thy memory not only the pot of manna, the bread of life; but even Aaron's rod, the very scourge of correction, wherewith you have been bettered. Blessed be the Lord, not only giving, but taking away, said Job. (See Job 1:21.) God, who sees there is no walking upon roses to heaven, puts His children into the way of discipline and by the fire of correction eats out the rust of corruption. God sends trouble; then He bids us call upon Him; He promises our deliverance; and lastly, the all [the only thing] He requires of us is to glorify Him. *"Call upon me in the day of trouble: I will deliver thee, and thou shalt glorify me"* (Ps. 50:15).

Like the nightingale, we can sing in the night, and we can say with John Newton,

> Since all that I meet shall work for my good,
> The bitter is sweet, the medicine food;
> Though painful at present, 'twill cease before
>   long,
> And then—oh, how pleasant!—the conqueror's
>   song.

Among all the apostles, none suffered as much as Paul, but none of them do we find giving thanks as often as he. Take his letter to the Philippians for an example. Remember what he suffered at Philippi, how they beat him with many blows and cast him into prison. Yet every chapter in this epistle speaks of rejoicing and giving thanks. There is this well-known passage:

Be careful for nothing; but in every thing by prayer and supplication with thanksgiving let your requests be made known unto God.
(Phil. 4:6)

As someone once said, there are, in this verse, three precious ideas: "Careful for nothing; prayerful for everything; and thankful for anything." We always get more by being thankful for what God has done for us.

Paul also said, *"We give thanks to God and the Father of our Lord Jesus Christ, praying always for you"* (Col. 1:3). He was constantly giving thanks. Look at any one of his epistles, and you will find them full of praise to God.

Even if we had nothing else to be thankful for, we would always have ample cause for giving thanks in that Jesus Christ loved us and gave Himself for us (Gal. 2:20).

A farmer was once found kneeling at a soldier's grave near Nashville. Someone came to him and said, "Why do you pay so much attention to this grave? Was your son buried here?"

"No," he said. "During the war my family were all sick; I knew not how I could leave them. I was drafted. One of my neighbors came over

71

and said, 'I will go for you; I have no family.' He went off. He was wounded at Chickamauga. He was carried to the hospital and there died. And, sir, I have come many miles so that I might write over his grave these words: 'He died for me.'"

Believers can always say of our blessed Savior the same thing, and we can greatly rejoice in this fact. *"By him therefore let us offer the sacrifice of praise to God continually, that is, the fruit of our lips giving thanks to his name"* (Heb. 13:15).

Pardon

Now, oh joy! My sins are pardoned!
    Now I can and do believe!
All I have, and am, and shall be,
    To my precious Lord I give;
He roused my deathly slumbers,
    He dispersed my soul's dark night,
Whispered peace and drew me to Him,
    Made Himself my chief delight.

Let the babe forget its mother,
    Let the bridegroom slight his bride;
True to Him, I'll love none other,
    Cleaving closely to His side.
Jesus, hear my soul's confession;
    Weak am I, but strength is Thine;
On Thine arms for strength and succor
    Calmly may my soul recline!

—Albert Midlane

CHAPTER 6

Forgiveness

The next thing is perhaps the most difficult of all to deal with—forgiveness. I believe this keeps more people from having power with God than any other—they are not willing to cultivate the spirit of forgiveness. If we allow the root of bitterness to spring up (Heb. 12:15) in our hearts against someone, our prayers will not be answered. It may not be an easy thing to live in sweet fellowship with all those with whom we come in contact, but that is why we are given the grace of God.

The Lord's Prayer, or, as I prefer to call it, the Disciples' Prayer, is a test of sonship; if we can pray it from the heart, we have good reason to think that we have been born of God. No one can call God "Father" except by the Spirit. (See Galatians 4:6–7.) Though this prayer has been such a blessing to the world, I believe it has been a great snare; many stumble over it into perdition. They do not weigh its meaning or take its facts right into their hearts.

I have no sympathy with the idea of universal sonship—that all men are the sons of God. The Bible teaches very plainly that we are adopted

into the family of God. (See Romans 8:15, Galatians 4:4–6, and Ephesians 1:5.) If all were sons,
God would not need to adopt any. We are all
God's by creation; but when people teach that
any man can say, *"Our Father which art in
heaven"* (Matt. 6:9) whether he is born of God or
not, I think that is contrary to Scripture.

*"As many as are led by the Spirit of God, they
are the sons of God"* (Rom. 8:14). Sonship in
God's family is the privilege of the believer. The
apostle John said, *"In this the children of God are
manifest, and the children of the devil"* (1 John
3:10). If we are doing the will of God, that is a
very good sign that we are born of God. If we
have no desire to do that will, how can we call
God *"our Father"*?

Also, we cannot really pray for God's kingdom to come until we are in it. If we should pray
for the coming of God's kingdom while we are
rebelling against Him, we are only seeking our
own condemnation. No unrenewed man really
wants God's will to be done on the earth. You
might write over the door of every unsaved
man's house, and over his place of business,
"God's will is not done here."

If the nations were really to pray this prayer,
all their armies could be discharged. I am told
there are some twelve million men in the standing armies of Europe alone. However, men do not
want God's will done on earth as it is in heaven;
that is the trouble.

Now let us come to the part I want to dwell
upon: *"Forgive us our debts, as we forgive our
debtors"* (Matt. 6:12). This is the only part of the
prayer that Christ explained:

*For if ye forgive men their trespasses, your
heavenly Father will also forgive you: but if
ye forgive not men their trespasses, neither
will your Father forgive your trespasses.*
(Matt. 6:14–15)

Notice that when you go into God's kingdom,
you go in through the door of forgiveness. I never
knew of a man getting a blessing in his own soul
if he was not willing to forgive others. If we are
unwilling to forgive others, God cannot forgive
us. I do not know how language could be clearer
than it is in these words of our Lord.

I firmly believe that many prayers are not
answered because we are not willing to forgive
someone. Let your mind go back over the past
and through the circle of your acquaintance. Are
there any against whom you are cherishing hard
feelings? Is there *"any root of bitterness springing
up"* (Heb. 12:15) against someone who has perhaps injured you? It may be that for months or
years you have been nursing this unforgiving
spirit; how can you ask God to forgive you? If I
am not willing to forgive those who may have
committed some single offense against me, what
a mean, contemptible thing it would be for me to
ask God to forgive the ten thousand sins of
which I have been guilty!

However, Christ went still further. He said,

*If thou bring thy gift to the altar, and there
rememberest that thy brother hath ought
against thee; leave there thy gift before the
altar, and go thy way; first be reconciled to
thy brother, and then come and offer thy
gift.*   (Matt. 5:23–24)

It may be that you are saying, "I do not know that I have anything against anyone." Has anyone anything against you? Is there someone who thinks you have done him wrong? Perhaps you have not, but it may be he thinks you have. I will tell you what I would do before I go to sleep tonight; I would go and see him and have the question settled. You will find that you will be greatly blessed in the very act. Suppose you are in the right and he is in the wrong; you may win your brother or sister. (See Matthew 18:15.) May God root out of all our hearts this unforgiving spirit.

A gentleman came to me some time ago and wanted me to talk to his wife about her soul. That woman seemed as apprehensive as any person I ever met, and I thought it would not take long to lead her into the light. However, it seemed that the longer I talked with her, the more her darkness increased. I went to see her again the next day and found her in still greater darkness of soul. I thought there must be something in the way that I had not discovered, and I asked her to repeat with me this Disciples' Prayer. I thought if she could say this prayer from the heart, the Lord would meet her in peace. I began to repeat it sentence after sentence, and she repeated it after me until I came to this petition: *"Forgive us our debts, as we forgive our debtors"* (Matt. 6:12). There she stopped. I repeated it the second time and waited for her to say it after me; she said she could not do it.

"What is the trouble?"

She replied, "There is one woman I never will forgive."

"Oh," I said, "I have discovered your difficulty; it is no use my going on to pray, for your prayers will not go higher than my head. God says He will not forgive you unless you forgive others. If you do not forgive this woman, God will never forgive you. That is the decree of heaven."

She said, "Do you mean to say that I cannot be forgiven until I have forgiven her?"

"No, I do not say it; the Lord says it, and that is far better authority."

Said she, "Then I will never be forgiven."

I left the house without having made any impression on her. A few years later, I heard that this woman was in an asylum for the insane. I believe this spirit of unforgiveness drove her mad.

If there is someone who has something against you, go at once and be reconciled. If you have something against anyone, write him a letter, telling him that you forgive him, and so have this thing off your conscience.

I remember being in the inquiry room[4] some years ago. I was in one corner of the room, talking to a young lady. There seemed to be something in the way, but I could not find out what it was. At last I said, "Isn't there someone you have not forgiven?"

She looked up at me and said, "What made you ask that? Has anyone told you about me?"

"No," I said, "but I thought perhaps that might be the case, since you have not received forgiveness yourself."

---

[4] Inquiry room: where seeking sinners were led after the meeting to ask questions about the Gospel and to receive Christ.

79

"Well," she said, pointing to another corner of the room, where there was a young lady sitting, "I have had trouble with that young lady; we have not spoken to each other for a long time."

"Oh," I said, "it is all plain to me now; you cannot be forgiven until you are willing to forgive her." It was a great struggle. But, you know, the greater the cross, the greater the blessing. It is human to err, but it is Christlike to forgive and be forgiven. At last this young lady said, "I will go and forgive her." Strange to say, the same conflict was going on in the mind of the lady in the other part of the room. They both came to their right minds about the same time. They met each other in the middle of the floor. Each tried to say that she forgave the other, but they could not finish; so they rushed into each other's arms. Then the four of us, the two seekers and the two workers, got down on our knees together, and we had a grand meeting. These two went away rejoicing.

Dear friend, is this the reason why your prayers are not answered? Is there some friend, some family member, someone in the church, you have not forgiven? We sometimes hear of members of the same church who have not spoken to each other for years. How can we expect God to forgive when this is the case?

I remember one town that Mr. Sankey[5] and I visited. For a week it seemed as if we were beating the air; there was no power in the meetings.

---

[5] Sankey: Ira Sankey, who assisted Moody by leading the singing in his meetings.

At last, one day I said that perhaps there was someone cultivating an unforgiving spirit. The chairman of our committee, who was sitting next to me, got up and left the meeting right in view of the audience. The arrow had hit the mark and gone home to the heart of the chairman of the committee. He had had trouble with someone for about six months. He at once hunted up this man and asked him to forgive him. He came to me with tears in his eyes and said, "I thank God you came here." That night the inquiry room was thronged. The chairman became one of the best workers I have ever known, and he has been active in Christian service ever since.

Several years ago the Church of England sent a devoted missionary to New Zealand. After a few years of toil and success, he was holding a communion service one Sunday in a district where the converts had not long since been savages. As the missionary was conducting the service, he observed one of the men—just as he was about to kneel at the rail—suddenly start to his feet and hastily go the opposite end of the church. By and by he returned and calmly took his place. After the service, the clergyman took him to one side and asked the reason for his strange behavior.

He replied, "As I was about to kneel, I recognized the man next to me. He was the chief of a neighboring tribe who had murdered my father and drunk his blood, and I had sworn by all the gods that I would slay that man at the first opportunity. At first, the impulse to have my revenge almost overpowered me, and I rushed away, as you saw me, to escape the power of it. As I stood at the other end of the room and considered the Object of our meeting, I thought of Christ as He prayed for His own murderers, *'Father, forgive them; for they know not what they do'* (Luke 23:34). I then felt that I could forgive the murderer of my father, and I came and knelt down at his side."

As someone once said, "There is an ugly kind of forgiveness in the world—a kind of hedgehog forgiveness, shot out like quills. A man takes one who has offended him and sets him down before the torch of his indignation, scorches him, and burns his fault into him; and when he has kneaded him sufficiently with his fists, then he forgives him."

The father of Frederick the Great, on his deathbed, was warned by M. Roloff, his spiritual adviser, that he was commanded to forgive his enemies. He was quite troubled, and after a moment's pause he said to the queen, "You, Feekin, may write to your brother (the King of England) *after I am dead* and tell him that I forgave him and died at peace with him." Upon hearing the statement, M. Roloff mildly suggested, "It would be better that Your Majesty write at once." "No," was the stern reply. "Write after I am dead. That will be safer."

Another story tells of a man who, supposing he was about to die, expressed his forgiveness to one who had injured him, but he added, "Now you mind, if I get well, the old grudge still stands."

My friends, that is not forgiveness at all. I believe true forgiveness includes forgetting the offense—putting it entirely out of our hearts and memories.

As Matthew Henry said,

> We do not forgive our offending brother aright nor acceptably if we do not forgive him from the heart, for it is the heart that God looks at. No malice must be harbored there, nor ill will to any; no projects of revenge must be hatched there, nor desires of it, as there are in many who outwardly appear peaceful and reconciled. We must from the heart desire and seek the welfare of those who have offended us.

If God's forgiveness were like the forgiveness often shown by us, it would not be worth much. Suppose God said, "I will forgive you, but I will never forget it; all through eternity I will keep reminding you of it." We would not look at that as forgiveness at all. Notice what God says: *"I will remember their sin no more"* (Jer. 31:34). In Ezekiel 33:16, it is said that not one of our sins will be mentioned; is that not like God? I do like to preach this forgiveness—the sweet truth that sin is blotted out for time and eternity and will never once be mentioned against us.

In another Scripture we read, *"Their sins and iniquities will I remember no more"* (Heb. 10:17). Then, when you turn to the eleventh chapter of Hebrews and read God's roll of honor, you find that not one of the sins of any of those men of faith is mentioned. Abraham is spoken of as the man of faith, but it is not told how he denied his wife down in Egypt; all that had been forgiven. Moses was kept out of the Promised Land because he had lost his patience, but this is not mentioned in the New Testament, though his name appears in the apostle's roll of honor. Samson, too, is named, but his sins are not brought up again. Why, the Bible even calls Lot a *"righteous man"* (2 Pet. 2:8); he did not look much like a righteous man in the Old Testament story, but he had been forgiven and had been made righteous by God. If we are once forgiven by God, our sins will be remembered against us no more. This is God's eternal decree.

Brooks said this of God's pardon granted to His people:

> When God pardons sin, He takes it sheer away; if it should be sought for, yet it could not be found, as the prophet Jeremiah speaks, *"In those days, and in that time, saith the* LORD, *the iniquity of Israel shall be sought for, and there shall be none; and the sins of Judah, and they shall not be found: for I will pardon them whom I reserve"* (Jer. 50:20). As David, when he saw in Mephibosheth the features of his friend Jonathan, took no notice of his lameness or any other defect or deformity, so God, beholding in His people the glorious image of His Son, winks at all their faults and deformities, which made Luther say, "Do with me what Thou wilt, since Thou hast pardoned my sin." And what is it to pardon sin, but to not mention sin?

We read in the gospel of Matthew,

> *Moreover if thy brother shall trespass against thee, go and tell him his fault between thee and him alone: if he shall hear thee, thou hast gained thy brother.* (Matt. 18:15)

Then a little further on we read that Peter came to Christ and said, *"How oft shall my brother sin against me, and I forgive him? till seven times?"* (Matt. 18:21). Jesus replied, *"I say not unto thee, Until seven times: but, Until seventy times seven"* (Matt. 18:22). Peter did not seem to think that he was in danger of falling into sin; his question was, "How often should I forgive my brother?" However, very soon we read that Peter did fall. I can imagine that when he fell, the sweet thought came to him of what the Master had said about forgiving seventy times seven. The voice of sin may be loud, but the voice of forgiveness is louder.

Let us enter into David's experience, when he said,

> *Blessed is he whose transgression is forgiven, whose sin is covered. Blessed is the man unto whom the LORD imputeth not iniquity, and in whose spirit there is no guile. When I kept silence, my bones waxed old through my roaring all the day long. For day and night thy hand was heavy upon me: my moisture is turned into the drought of summer. Selah. I acknowledged my sin unto thee, and mine iniquity have I not hid. I said, I will confess my transgressions unto the LORD; and thou forgavest the iniquity of my sin.* (Ps. 32:1–5)

David could look behind, below, above, and before—to the past, present, and future—and know that all was well. Let us make up our minds that we will not rest until this question of sin is forever settled so that we can look up and claim God as our forgiving Father. Let us be willing to forgive others so that we may be able to claim forgiveness from God, remembering the words of the Lord Jesus, how He said,

> *If ye forgive men their trespasses, your heavenly Father will also forgive you: but if ye forgive not men their trespasses, neither will your Father forgive your trespasses.*
>
> (Matt. 6:14–15)

Union

Let party names no more be known
    Among the ransomed throng;
For Jesus claims them for His own;
    To Him they all belong.

One in their covenant Head and King,
    They should be one in heart;
Of one salvation all should sing,
    Each claiming his own part.

One bread, one family, one rock,
    One building, formed by love,
One fold, one Shepherd, yea, one flock,
    They shall be one above.

—Joseph Irons

CHAPTER 7

Unity

The next thing we need to have, if we want to get our prayers answered, is unity. If we do not love one another, we certainly will not have much power with God in prayer. One of the saddest things in the present day is the division in God's church. Notice that when the power of God came upon the early church, it was when they were all in one accord. (See Acts 2:1.) I believe that the blessing of Pentecost would never have been given if it had not been for that spirit of unity. If they had been divided and quarreling among themselves, do you think the Holy Spirit would have come, and do you think those thousands would have been converted?

I have noticed in our work that, when we go to a town where three churches are united, we have greater blessing than when only one church is in harmony; and when there are twelve churches united, the blessing is multiplied fourfold. The results are always in proportion to the spirit of unity that is manifested. Where there are bickerings and division and where the spirit of unity is absent, there is very little blessing and praise.

Dr. Guthrie illustrated this fact when he said,

> Separate the atoms which make the hammer, and each would fall on the stone as a snowflake; but welded into one, and wielded by the firm arm of the quarryman, it will break the massive rocks asunder. Divide the waters of Niagara into distinct and individual drops, and they would be no more than the falling rain, but in their united body they would quench the fires of Vesuvius and have some to spare for the volcanoes of other mountains.

History tells us that the Roman and the Alban armies agreed to settle their dispute by a battle between six brothers—three on the one side, the sons of Curatius, and three on the other, the sons of Horatius. While the Curatii were united, though all three were severely wounded, they killed two of the Horatii. The third began to take to his heels, though not hurt at all; but when he saw them following slowly, one after another because of wounds and heavy armor, he fell upon them singly and slew all three. It is the cunning trick of the devil to divide us so that he may destroy us.

We ought to endure much and sacrifice much rather than permit discord and division to prevail in our hearts. Martin Luther said,

> When two goats meet upon a narrow bridge over deep water, how do they behave? Neither of them can turn back again; neither can pass the other, because the bridge is too narrow. If they should thrust one another, they might both fall into the

water and be drowned. Nature, then, has taught them that if the one lays himself down and permits the other to go over him, both remain unhurt. Even so, people should rather endure to be trod upon than to fall into debate and discord one with another.

Cawdray said,

As in music, if the harmony of tones is not complete, they are offensive to the cultivated ear; so if Christians disagree among themselves, they are unacceptable to God.

Paul wrote, *"Now there are diversities of gifts, but the same Spirit. And there are differences of administrations, but the same Lord"* (1 Cor. 12:4–5). There are diversities of gifts—that is clearly taught—but there is one Spirit. If we have all been redeemed with the same blood, we ought to see eye to eye in spiritual things.

Where there is union, I do not believe any power, earthly or infernal, can stand before the work. When the church, both the pulpit and the pew, get united, and God's people are all of one mind, Christianity is like a red-hot ball rolling over the earth, and all the hosts of death and hell cannot stand before it. I believe that men will then come flocking into the kingdom by hundreds and thousands. *"By this,"* says Christ, *"shall all men know that ye are my disciples, if ye have love one to another"* (John 13:35). If we only love one another and pray for one another, there will be success. God will not disappoint us.

There can be no real separation or division in the true church of Christ because believers are redeemed by one price and indwelt by one Spirit. If I belong to the family of God, I have been bought with the same blood as any other child of God, though I may not belong to the same sect or party. What we need is to get these miserable sectarian walls taken away. Our weakness has been in our division, and what we need is to have no schism or division among those who love the Lord Jesus Christ. In the first epistle to the Corinthians, we read about the first symptoms of sectarianism in the early church:

> Now I beseech you, brethren, by the name of our Lord Jesus Christ, that ye all speak the same thing, and that there be no divisions among you; but that ye be perfectly joined together in the same mind and in the same judgment. For it hath been declared unto me of you, my brethren, by them which are of the house of Chloe, that there are contentions among you. Now this I say, that every one of you saith, I am of Paul; and I of Apollos; and I of Cephas; and I of Christ. Is Christ divided? was Paul crucified for you? or were ye baptized in the name of Paul?
>
> (1 Cor. 1:10–13)

Notice how one said, "I am with Paul," and another, "I am with Apollos," and another, "I am with Cephas." Apollos was a young orator, and some had been carried away by his eloquence. Others favored Cephas, or Peter, saying he was of the regular apostolic line, because he had been with the Lord, whereas Paul had not. Hence, they were divided, and Paul wrote this letter in order to settle the question.

Jenkyn, in his commentary on the epistle of Jude, said,

> The partakers of a "common salvation," who here agree about the one way to heaven, and who expect to be, hereafter, in one heaven, should be of one heart. It is the apostle's inference in Ephesians. What an amazing misery it is, that they who agree in common faith should disagree like common foes! That Christians should live as if faith had banished love! This common faith should allay and temper our spirits in all our differences. This should moderate our minds, though there is inequality in earthly relations. What powerful motive Joseph had to forgive his brothers, they being both his brothers and the servants of the God of his fathers! Though our own breath cannot blow out the taper [candle] of contention, oh, let the blood of Christ extinguish it!

What a strange state of things Paul, Cephas, and Apollos would find if they were to come to the world today! The little tree that sprang up at Corinth has grown up into a tree like Nebuchadnezzar's, with many of the fowls of heaven gathered on it. (See Daniel 4:10–12.)

Suppose Paul and Cephas were to come down to us now; they would hear at once about our Churchmen and Dissenters.[6] "A Dissenter!" Paul would say. "What is that?"

---

[6] Dissenter: a Presbyterian who refused to agree with the doctrines of the Established Church in England.

"We have a Church of England, and there are those who dissent from the Church."

"Oh, indeed! Are there two classes of Christians here, then?"

"I am sorry to say there are many more divisions. The Dissenters themselves are split up. There are Wesleyans, Baptists, Presbyterians, Independents, and so on; even these are all divided up."

"Can it be possible," Paul would say, "that there are so many divisions?"

"Yes, the Church of England is pretty well divided itself. There is the Broad Church, the High Church, the Low Church, and the High-Lows. Then there is the Lutheran Church, and away in Russia they have the Greek Church, and so on."

I declare I do not know what Paul and Cephas would think if they came back to the world; they would find a strange state of things. It is one of the most humiliating things in the present day to see how God's family is divided up. If we love the Lord Jesus Christ, the burden of our hearts will be that God may bring us closer together, so that we may love one another and rise above all party feelings.

When a church in one of the Boston wards was repaired, the inscription upon the wall behind the pulpit was covered up. The inscription had read, *"A new commandment I give unto you, That ye love one another"* (John 13:34). Upon the first Sunday after repairs, a little five-year-old whispered to her mother, "I know why God told the painters to cover that pretty verse up. It was because the people don't love one another."

A Boston minister said he once preached on "The Recognition of Friends in the Future," and was told after the service by a hearer that it would be more to the point to preach about the recognition of friends here, as he had been in the church for twenty years and did not know any of its members.

I was in a little town some time ago when one night, as I came out of the church meeting, I saw another building where people were coming out. I said to a friend, "Have you got two churches here?"

"Oh yes."

"How do you get along?"

"Oh, we get along very well."

"I'm glad to hear that. Has the other church's minister been to your meetings?"

"Oh no, these two churches don't have anything to do with each other. We find that is the best way."

"Getting along very well" was what he called that! Oh, may God make us of one heart and of one mind! Let our hearts be like drops of water flowing together. Unity among the people of God is a sort of foretaste of heaven. There we will not find any Baptists or Methodists or Congregationalists or Episcopalians; we will all be one in Christ. We leave all our party names behind us when we leave this earth. May the Spirit of God speedily sweep away all these miserable walls that we have been building up!

Did you ever notice that the last prayer Jesus Christ made on earth, before He was led away to Calvary, was that His disciples might all be one? (See John 17:21.) He could look down the stream of time and see that divisions would come, that Satan would try to divide the flock of God.

Nothing will silence infidels so quickly as Christians everywhere being united. Then our testimony will have weight with the ungodly and the careless. However, when they see how Christians are divided, they will not believe their testimony. The Holy Spirit is grieved, and there is little power, where there is no unity.

If I thought I had one drop of sectarian blood in my veins, I would bleed it out before I went to bed; if I had one sectarian hair in my head, I would pull it out before I went to sleep. Let us get right to the heart of Jesus Christ; then our prayers will be acceptable to God, and showers of blessings will descend.

Have Faith in God

Have faith in God, for He who reigns on high
Hath borne thy grief, and hears the suppliant's sigh;
Still to His arms, thine only refuge, fly,
    Have faith in God!

Fear not to call on Him, O soul distressed!
Thy sorrow's whisper woos thee to His breast;
He who is oftenest there is oftenest blest.
    Have faith in God!

Lean not on Egypt's reeds; slake not thy thirst
At earthly cisterns. Seek the Kingdom first.
Though man and Satan fright thee with their worst,
    Have faith in God!

Go, tell Him all! The sigh thy bosom heaves
Is heard in heaven. Strength and peace He gives,
Who gave Himself for thee. Our Jesus lives;
    Have faith in God!

—*Anna Shipton*

CHAPTER 8

Faith

Another essential element of prayer is faith. It is as important for us to know how to pray as it is to know how to work. We are not told that Jesus ever taught His disciples to preach, but He taught them how to pray. He wanted them to have power with God; He knew that they would then have power with man.

In James we read, *"If any of you lack wisdom, let him ask of God...and it shall be given him. But let him ask in faith, nothing wavering"* (James 1:5–6). Faith is the golden key that unlocks the treasures of heaven. It was the shield that David took when he met Goliath on the field; he believed that God was going to deliver the Philistine into his hands. Someone once said that faith could lead Christ anywhere; wherever He found it, He honored it. Unbelief sees something in God's hand and says, "I cannot get it." Faith sees it and says, "I will have it."

The new life begins with faith; then we only have to continue building on that foundation. *"I say unto you, What things soever ye desire, when ye pray, believe that ye receive them, and ye shall have them"* (Mark 11:24). However, bear in mind, we must be in earnest when we go to God.

The following story is an example of the distressed cry for help going up to God, in all the earnestness of deeply realized need; I do not know of a more vivid illustration. Carl Steinman, who visited Mount Hecla, Iceland, just before it erupted in 1845 after a repose of eighty years, narrowly escaped death after venturing into the smoking crater against the earnest entreaty of his guide. He was thrown down on the brink of the yawning gulf by a convulsion of the summit and held there by blocks of lava upon his feet. He graphically wrote of that perilous situation:

> Oh, the horrors of that awful realization! There, over the mouth of a black and heated abyss, I was held suspended, a helpless and conscious prisoner, to be hurled downward by the next great throe of trembling Nature!
>
> "Help! Help! Help!—for the love of God, help!" I shrieked, in the very agony of my despair.
>
> I had nothing to rely upon but the mercy of heaven; and I prayed to God as I had never prayed before, for the forgiveness of my sins, that they might not follow me to judgment.
>
> All at once I heard a shout, and, looking around, I beheld, with feelings that cannot be described, my faithful guide hastening down the sides of the crater to my relief.
>
> "I warned you!" said he.
>
> "You did!" cried I, "But forgive me, and save me, for I am perishing!"
>
> "I will save you or perish with you!"

The earth trembled, and the rocks parted—one of them rolling down the chasm with a dull, booming sound. I sprang forward; I seized a hand of the guide, and the next moment we had both fallen, locked in each other's arms, upon the solid earth above. I was free, but still upon the verge of the pit.

Bishop Hall, in a well-known extract, thus explained the relationship between earnestness and the prayer of faith:

An arrow, if it is drawn back but a little way, goes not far; but, if it is pulled back to the head, flies swiftly and pierces deeply. Thus prayer, if it is only dribbled forth from careless lips, falls at our feet. It is the strength of exclamation and strong desire which sends it to heaven and makes it pierce the clouds. It is not the arithmetic of our prayers, how many they may be; nor the rhetoric of our prayers, how eloquent they may be; nor the geometry of our prayers, how long they may be; nor the music of our prayers, how sweet our voice may be; nor the logic of our prayers, how argumentative they may be; nor the method of our prayers, how orderly they may be; nor even the divinity of our prayers, how good the doctrine may be; it is none of these things which God cares for. He looks not for the calloused knees which James is said to have had through the assiduity of prayer.

We might be like Bartholomew, who is said to have had a hundred prayers for the morning, and as many for the evening, and all might be of no avail. Fervency of spirit is that which availeth much.

Archbishop Leighton said,

It is not the gilded paper and good writing of a petition that prevails with a king, but the moving sense of it. And to that King who discerns the heart, heart-sense is the sense of all, and that which He regards alone. He listens to hear what that speaks and takes all as nothing where that is silent. All other excellence in prayer is but the outside and fashion of it. This is the life of it.

Brooks said,

As a painted fire is no fire, and a dead man no man, so a cold prayer is no prayer. In a painted fire there is no heat, in a dead man there is no life; so in a cold prayer there is no potency, no devotion, no blessing. Cold prayers are as arrows without heads, as swords without edges, as birds without wings; they pierce not, they cut not, they fly not up to heaven. Cold prayers always freeze before they get to heaven. Oh, that Christians would chide themselves out of their cold prayers, and chide themselves into a better and warmer frame of spirit, when they make their supplications to the Lord!

Take the case of the Syrophenician woman. When she called to the Master, it seemed for a time as if He were deaf to her request. The disciples wanted her to be sent away. Although they were with Christ for three years and sat at His feet, they did not know how full of grace His heart was. Think of Christ sending away a poor sinner who had come to Him for mercy! Can you conceive of such a thing? Never once did it occur. This poor woman put herself in the place of her child. She cried, *"Lord, help me!"* (Matt. 15:25). I think when we get that far in our desire to have our friends blessed—when we put ourselves in their place—God will soon hear our prayer.

A number of years ago at a meeting, I remember I asked all those who wished to become Christians to come forward and kneel or take seats in the front. Among those who came was a woman whom I thought, by her looks, must be a Christian, but she knelt down with the others. I said, "You are a Christian, are you not?" She said she had been one for a certain number of years. "Did you understand the invitation? I asked only those who wanted to become Christians." I will never forget the look on her face as she replied, "I have a son who has gone far away; I thought I would take his place today and see if God would not bless him." Thank God for such a mother as that!

The Syrophenician woman did the same thing: *"Lord, help me!"* It was a short prayer, but it went right to the heart of the Son of God. He tried her faith, however:

> *But he answered and said, It is not meet to take the children's bread, and cast it to dogs. And she said, Truth, Lord: yet the*

dogs eat of the crumbs which fall from their masters' table. Then Jesus answered and said unto her, O woman, great is thy faith.
(Matt. 15:26–28)

What a testimonial He paid to her! Her story will never be forgotten as long as the church is on the earth. He honored her faith, and He gave her all she asked for.

Everyone can say, *"Lord, help me!"* We all need help. As Christians, we need more grace, more love, more purity of life, more righteousness. Then let us make this prayer today. I want God to help me to preach better and to live better, to be more like the Son of God. The golden chains of faith link us right to the throne of God, and the grace of heaven flows down into our souls.

As far as I know, that woman might have been a great sinner; the Lord still heard her cry. It may be that, up to this hour, you have been living in sin; but if you will cry, *"Lord, help me!"* He will answer your prayer, if it is an honest one.

Very often we do not really mean anything when we cry to God. You mothers understand that. Your children have two voices. When they ask you for something, you can soon tell if the cry is a make-believe one or not. If it is, you do not give any heed to it; but if it is a real cry for help, how quickly you respond! The cry of distress always brings relief.

For instance, your child is playing, and he says, "Mamma, I want some bread," but goes on playing. Knowing that he is not very hungry, you let him alone. By and by, however, the child drops the toys and comes tugging at your clothes. "Mamma, I am so hungry!" Then you know that the cry is a real one; you quickly go to the pantry and get some bread. Likewise, when we are in earnest for the bread of heaven, we will get it. The Syrophenician woman was terribly in earnest; therefore, her petition was answered.

I remember hearing of a boy brought up in an English poorhouse. He had never learned to read or write, except that he could read the letters of the alphabet. One day a man of God came there, and he told the children that if they would pray to God in their trouble, He would send them help. After a time, this boy was apprenticed to a farmer. One day he was sent out into the fields to look after some sheep. He was having rather a hard time of it, but he remembered what the preacher had said. He decided to pray to God about it. Someone going by the field heard a voice behind the hedge. He looked to see whose it was, and he saw the little fellow on his knees, saying, "A, B, C, D," and so on.

The man said, "My boy, what are you doing?" He looked up and said he was praying. "Why, that is not praying; it is only reciting the alphabet." He said he did not know just how to pray, but there once came to the poorhouse a man who told them that if they called upon God, He would help them. So he thought that if he recited the letters of the alphabet, God would take them and put them together into a prayer and give him what he needed. The little fellow was really praying.

Sometimes, when your child talks, your friends cannot understand what he says, but you understand very well. If our prayer comes right from the heart, God understands our language. It is a delusion of the devil to think we cannot pray; we can, if we really want something. It is not the most beautiful or the most eloquent language that brings down the answer; it is the cry that goes up from a burdened heart. When this poor Gentile woman cried out, *"Lord, help me!"* the cry flashed over the divine wires, and the blessing came. So you can pray if you will; it is the desire, the wish of the heart, that God delights to hear and to answer.

In addition to being earnest, we must be expectant—we must expect to receive a blessing. When the centurion wanted Christ to heal his servant, he thought he was not worthy to go and ask the Lord himself, so he sent his friends to make the petition. He sent out messengers to meet the Master and say, "Don't trouble Yourself to come; all You have to do is to speak the word, and the disease will go." (See Luke 7:6–7.) Jesus said to the Jews, *"I have not found so great faith, no, not in Israel"* (Luke 7:9). He marveled at the faith of this centurion; it pleased Him so much that He healed the servant right then. Faith brought the answer.

In John's gospel, we read of a nobleman whose child was sick. The father fell on his knees before the Master and said, *"Come down ere my child die"* (John 4:49). Here you have both earnestness and faith, and the Lord answered the prayer at once. The man's son began to recover that very hour. Christ honored the man's faith.

In his case, there was nothing to rest upon but the bare word of Christ, but this was enough. It is good to always bear in mind that the object of faith is not the creature, but the Creator; not the instrument, but the Hand that wields it.

Richard Sibbes put it this way for us:

The object in believing is God, and Christ as Mediator. We must have both to found our faith upon. We cannot believe in God except we believe in Christ. For God must be satisfied by God; and by Him that is God must that satisfaction be applied— the Spirit of God. He works faith in the heart and raises it up when it is dejected.

All is supernatural in faith. The things we believe are above nature; the promises are above nature; the worker of it, the Holy Spirit, is above nature; and everything in faith is above nature.

There must be a God in whom we believe, and a God through whom we may know that Christ is God—not only by that which Christ has done, the miracles, which none could do but God, but also by what is done to Him. And two things are done to Him, which show that He is God—that is, faith and prayer. We must believe only in God and pray only to God; but Christ is the object of both of these. He is set forth as the object of faith and of prayer in the prayer of Saint Stephen, *"Lord Jesus, receive my spirit"* (Acts 7:59). And, therefore, He is God; for that is done unto Him which is proper and peculiar only to God.

Oh, what a strong foundation, what bottom and basis our faith has! There is

God the Father, Son, and Holy Spirit, and Christ the Mediator. That our faith may be supported, we have Him to believe on who supports heaven and earth.

There is nothing that can lie in the way of the accomplishment of any of God's promises that is not conquerable by faith.

Samuel Rutherford, a Scottish preacher, said this about the Syrophenician woman:

See the sweet use of faith under a sad temptation; faith barters with Christ and heaven in the dark, upon plain trust and credit, without seeing any surety of dawn. *"Blessed are they that have not seen, and yet have believed"* (John 20:29). And the reason is that faith is sinewed and boned with spiritual courage, so as to keep a barred city against hell, yea, and to stand under impossibilities. Here is a weak woman, though not as a woman, yet as a believer, persisting with Him who is *"the Mighty God, the everlasting Father, the Prince of Peace."* (Isa. 9:6). Only faith persists, and overcometh the sword, the world, and all afflictions. This is our victory, whereby one man overcometh the great and vast world. [See 1 John 5:4.]

Bishop Ryle has taught that Christ's intercession is the ground and sureness of our faith:

The banknote without a signature at the bottom is nothing but a worthless piece of paper. The stroke of a pen confers on it all its value. The prayer of a poor child of

Faith

Adam is a feeble thing in itself, but once
endorsed by the hand of the Lord Jesus, it
avails much. There was an officer in the
city of Rome who was appointed to have
his doors always open in order to receive
any Roman citizen who applied to him for
help. Just so, the ear of the Lord Jesus is
ever open to the cry of all who want mercy
and grace. It is His office to help them.
Their prayer is His delight. Reader, think of
this. Is not this encouragement?

Let us close this chapter by referring to some
of our Lord's own words concerning faith in its
relation to prayer:

*And when he saw a fig tree in the way, he
came to it, and found nothing thereon, but
leaves only, and said unto it, Let no fruit
grow on thee henceforward for ever. And
presently the fig tree withered away. And
when the disciples saw it, they marvelled,
saying, How soon is the fig tree withered
away! Jesus answered and said unto them,
Verily I say unto you, If ye have faith, and
doubt not, ye shall not only do this which is
done to the fig tree, but also if ye shall say
unto this mountain, Be thou removed, and
be thou cast into the sea; it shall be done.
And all things, whatsoever ye shall ask in
prayer, believing, ye shall receive.*
(Matt. 21:19–22)

Moreover, our Lord said,

*Verily, verily, I say unto you, He that be-
lieveth on me, the works that I do shall he*

do also; and greater works than these shall he do; because I go unto my Father. And whatsoever ye shall ask in my name, that will I do, that the Father may be glorified in the Son. If ye shall ask any thing in my name, I will do it. (John 14:12–14)

If ye abide in me, and my words abide in you, ye shall ask what ye will, and it shall be done unto you. (John 15:7)

Verily, verily, I say unto you, Whatsoever ye shall ask the Father in my name, he will give it you. Hitherto have ye asked nothing in my name: ask, and ye shall receive, that your joy may be full. (John 16:23–24)

To See His Face

Sweet is the precious gift of prayer,
    To bow before a throne of grace;
To leave our every burden there,
    And gain new strength to run our race;
To gird our heavenly armor on,
Depending on the Lord alone.

And sweet the whisper of His love,
    When conscience sinks beneath its load,
That bids our guilty fears remove,
    And points to Christ's atoning blood;
Oh, then 'tis sweet indeed to know
God can be just and gracious too.

But oh, to see our Savior's face!
    From sin and sorrow to be freed!
To dwell in His divine embrace—
    This will be sweeter far indeed!
The fairest form of earthly bliss
Is less than nought, compared with this.

—Author Unknown

CHAPTER 9

Petition

The next element in prayer that I notice is petition. How often we go to prayer meetings without really asking for anything! Our prayers go all around the world, without anything definite being asked for. We do not expect anything. Many people would be greatly surprised if God did answer their prayers.

I remember hearing of a very eloquent man who was leading a meeting in prayer. There was not a single definite petition in his whole prayer. A poor, earnest woman shouted out, "Ask Him for something, man." How often you hear what is called prayer without any asking! *"Ask, and ye shall receive"* (John 16:24).

I believe if we get all the stumbling blocks out of the way, God will answer our petitions. If we put away sin and come into His presence with pure hands, as He has commanded us to come, our prayers will have power with Him. In Luke's gospel we have as a grand supplement to the Disciples' Prayer (see Luke 11:2–4) the following promise: *"Ask, and it shall be given you; seek, and ye shall find; knock, and it shall be opened unto you"* (Luke 11:9). Some people think God does not like to be troubled with our constant coming and asking. The only way to trouble God is not to come at all. He encourages us to come to Him repeatedly and press our claims.

I believe you will find three kinds of Christians in the church today. The first is those who ask; the second is those who seek; and the third is those who knock.

"Teacher," said a bright, earnest-faced boy, "why is it that so many prayers are unanswered? I do not understand. The Bible says, *'Ask, and it shall be given you; seek, and ye shall find; knock, and it shall be opened unto you'* (Luke 11:9); but it seems to me that many knock and are not admitted."

"Have you ever sat by your cheerful living room fire on some dark evening," said the teacher, "and heard a loud knock at the door? When you went to answer the door, did you peer out into the darkness, but saw nothing, yet you heard the pattering feet of some mischievous boy, who had knocked but did not wish to enter and so ran away? It is often thus with us. We ask for blessings but do not really expect them; we knock but do not plan to enter. We fear that Jesus will not hear us, will not fulfill His promises, will not admit us; and so we go away."

"Ah, I see," said the earnest-faced boy, his eyes shining with the new light dawning in his soul. "Jesus cannot be expected to answer runaway knocks. He has never promised it. I mean to keep knocking and knocking until He cannot help opening the door."

Too often we knock at mercy's door and then run away instead of waiting for an entrance and an answer. Thus, we act as if we were afraid of having our prayers answered.

Many people pray in that way; they do not wait for the answer. Our Lord is teaching us that we are not only to ask, but we are to wait for the answer. If it does not come, we must seek to find out the reason. I believe that we get a good number of blessings just by asking; others we do not get because there may be something in our lives that needs to be brought to light.

When Daniel began to pray in Babylon for the deliverance of his people, he sought to find out what the trouble was and why God had turned away His face from them. Likewise, there may be something in our lives that is keeping back the blessing; if there is, we need to find it.

Someone, speaking on this subject, has said, "We are to ask with a beggar's humility, to seek with a servant's carefulness, and to knock with the confidence of a friend."

How often people become discouraged and say they do not know whether God answers prayer! In the parable of the importunate widow (see Luke 18:2–8), Christ is teaching us how we are not only to pray and seek, but also to find. If the unjust judge heard the petition of the poor woman who pushed her claims, how much more will our heavenly Father hear our cry!

Many years ago in the state of New Jersey, an Irishman was condemned to be hanged. Every possible influence was brought to bear upon the governor to have the man reprieved, but he stood firm and refused to alter the sentence. One morning, the wife of the condemned man, with her ten children, went to see the governor. When he came to his office, they all fell on their faces before him and begged him to have mercy on the husband and father. The governor's heart was moved, and he at once wrote out a reprieve. The importunity of the wife and children saved the life of the man, just as the woman in the parable pressed her claims and induced the unjust judge to grant her request.

It was this same kind of persistence that brought the answer to the prayer of blind Bartimaeus. The people, and even the disciples, tried to hush him into silence; but he only cried out the louder, *"Thou Son of David, have mercy on me!"* (Mark 10:48).

Prayer is hardly ever mentioned in the Bible alone; it is prayer and earnestness, prayer and watchfulness, prayer and thanksgiving. We are instructed by the fact that, throughout Scripture, prayer is always linked with something else. Bartimaeus prayed earnestly, and the Lord heard his cry.

The highest type of Christian is the one who has gotten entirely beyond asking and seeking, and keeps on knocking until the answer comes. If we continue to knock, God has promised to open the door and grant our request. It may be years before the answer comes—He may keep us knocking—but He has promised that the answer will come.

I will tell you what I think it means to knock. A number of years ago, when we were having meetings in a certain city, it came to a point where there seemed to be very little power. We called together all the mothers and asked them to meet and pray for their children. About fifteen hundred mothers came together and poured out their hearts to God in prayer. One mother said, "I wish you would pray for my two boys. They have gone off on a drunken spree, and it seems as if my heart would break." She was a widowed mother. A few mothers gathered together and said, "Let us have a prayer meeting for these boys." They cried to God for these two wandering boys. Now see how God answered their prayer.

That day these two brothers had planned to meet at the corner of the street where our meetings were being held. They had planned to spend the night in debauchery and sin. About seven o'clock, the first one arrived at the appointed place; he saw people going into the meeting. Since it was a stormy night, he thought he would go in for a little while. The Word of God reached him, and he went into the inquiry room, where he gave his heart to the Savior.

The other brother waited at the corner until the meeting broke up, expecting his brother to come; he did not know that he had been in the meeting. There was another meeting for young men in the church nearby, and this brother thought he would like to see what was going on, so he followed the crowd into that meeting. He also was impressed with what he heard, and he was the first one to go into the inquiry room, where he found peace. While this was happening, the first one had gone home to cheer his mother's heart with the good news. He found her on her knees. She had been knocking at the mercy seat. While she was doing so, her boy came in and told her that her prayers had been answered; his soul was saved. It was not long before the other brother came in and told his story how he, too, had been blessed.

On the following Monday night, the first to get up at the young converts' meeting was one of these brothers, who told the story of their conversion. No sooner had he taken his seat than the other jumped up and said, "All that my brother has told you is true, for I am his brother. The Lord has indeed met us and blessed us."

I heard of a certain wife in England who had an unconverted husband. She resolved that she would pray every day for twelve months for his conversion. Every day at twelve o'clock, she went to her room alone and cried to God. Her husband would not allow her to speak to him on the subject, but she could speak to God on his behalf. (It may be that you have a friend who does not wish to be spoken to about his salvation; you can do as this woman did—go and pray to God about it.)

The twelve months went by, and there was no sign of his yielding. She resolved to pray for six months longer; every day she went alone and prayed for the conversion of her husband. The six months passed, and still there was no sign, no answer. The question arose in her mind, "Can I give up on him?" "No," she vowed, "I will pray for him as long as God gives me breath."

That very day, when he came home to dinner, instead of going into the dining room, he went upstairs. She waited and waited, but he did not come down to dinner. Finally, she went to his room and found him on his knees, crying to God to have mercy upon him. God had convicted him of sin; he not only became a Christian, but the Word of God had free course and was glorified in him. (See 2 Thessalonians 3:1.) God used him mightily. That was God answering the prayers of this Christian wife; she knocked and knocked until the answer came.

I heard a story once that cheered me greatly. Prayer had been made for a man for about forty years, but there was no sign of any answer. It seemed as though he would go down to his grave as one of the most self-righteous men on the face of the earth. Conviction, however, came in one night. In the morning, he sent for the members of his family and said to his daughter, "I want you to pray for me. Pray that God would forgive my sins; my whole life has been nothing but sin—sin." This conviction came all at once in one night.

What we need to do is press our case right up to the throne of God. I have often known cases of men who came to our meetings, and although they could not hear a word that was said, it seemed as though some unseen power laid hold of them so that they were convicted and converted then and there.

I remember at one place where we were holding meetings, a wife came to the first meeting and asked me to talk with her husband. "He is not interested," she said, "but I have hope that he will become interested." I talked with him, and I think I have rarely ever spoken to a man who seemed so self-righteous. It looked as though I might as well have talked to an iron post, so encased he seemed to be in self-righteousness. I told his wife that he was not at all interested. She said, "I told you that, but I am interested for him."

All the thirty days we were there, that wife never gave him up. I must confess she had ten times more faith for him than I had. I had spoken to him several times, but I could see no ray of hope. The third to last night, the man came to me and said, "Would you see me in another room?" I went aside with him and asked him what was the trouble. He said, "I am the greatest sinner in the state of Vermont." "How is that?" I asked. "Is there any particular sin you have been guilty of?" I must confess that I thought he had committed some awful crime that he had been covering up and that he now wanted to make confession.

"My whole life," he said, "has been nothing but sin. God has shown it to me today." He asked the Lord to have mercy on him, and he went home rejoicing in the assurance of sins forgiven. That was a man convicted and converted in answer to prayer.

If you are anxious about the conversion of some relative or friend, make up your mind that you will give God no rest, day or night, until He grants your petition. He can reach them, wherever they are—at their places of business, in their homes, or anywhere—and bring them to His feet.

Dr. Austin Phelps, in his "Still Hour," said,

> The prospect of gaining an object will always cause the expression of intense desire. The feeling—which will become spontaneous with a Christian under the influence of such a trust—is this: "I come to my devotions this morning on an errand of real life.

This is no romance and no farce. I do not come here to go through a form of words; I have no hopeless desires to express. I have an object to gain; I have an end to accomplish. This is a business in which I am about to engage. An astronomer does not turn his telescope to the skies with a more reasonable hope of penetrating those distant heavens than I have of reaching the mind of God by lifting up my heart at the throne of grace. This is the privilege of my calling of God in Christ Jesus. Even my faltering voice is now to be heard in heaven; and it is to put forth a new power there, the results of which only God can know and only eternity can develop. Therefore, O Lord, Thy servant finds it in his heart to pray this prayer unto Thee!"

Jeremy Taylor said,

Easiness of desire is a great enemy to the success of a good man's prayer. It must be an intent, zealous, busy, operative prayer; for consider what a huge indecency it is that a man should speak to God for a thing that he values not! Our prayers upbraid our spirits when we beg tamely for those things for which we ought to die, which are more precious than imperial scepters, richer than the spoils of the sea or the treasures of Indian hills.

Dr. Patton, in his work on "Remarkable Answers to Prayer," illustrated the folly of praying without expecting to receive an answer:

Jesus bids us seek. Imagine a mother seeking a lost child. She looks through the house and along the streets, searches the fields and woods, and examines the riverbanks. A [disillusioned] neighbor meets her and says, "Seek on, look everywhere; search every accessible place. You will not find, indeed; but then seeking is a good thing. It stretches the mind; it fixes the attention; it aids observation; it makes the idea of the child very real. And then, after a while, you will cease to want your child."

The words of Christ are, *"Knock, and it shall be opened unto you"* (Luke 11:9). Imagine a man knocking at the door of a house, long and loud. After he has done this for an hour, a window opens, and the occupant of the house puts out his head and says, "That is right, my friend; I shall not open the door, but keep on knocking—it is excellent exercise, and you will be the healthier for it. Knock away till sundown; and then come again, and knock all tomorrow. After some days thus spent, you will attain to a state of mind in which you will no longer care to come in." Is this what Jesus intended us to understand, when He said, *"Ask, and it shall be given you; seek, and ye shall find; knock, and it shall be opened unto you"* (Luke 11:9)? [Absolutely not!] No doubt, one would thus soon cease to ask, to seek, and to knock; but would it not be from disgust?

Nothing is more pleasing to our heavenly Father than direct, importunate, and persevering prayer. Two Christian ladies, whose husbands were unconverted, feeling their great danger, agreed to spend one hour each day in united prayer for their salvation. This was continued for seven years. At this time, they debated whether they should pray any longer, so useless did their prayers appear. They decided to persevere until death, and, if their husbands went to destruction, the way would be laden with prayers. In renewed strength, they prayed three years longer, when one of them was awakened in the night by her husband, who was in great distress for sin. As soon as the day dawned, she hastened with joy to tell her praying companion that God was about to answer their prayers. Imagine her surprise to meet her friend coming to her on the same errand! Thus, ten years of united and persevering prayer was crowned with the conversion of both husbands on the same day.

We cannot be too frequent in our requests; God will not weary of His children's prayers. Sir Walter Raleigh asked a favor of Queen Elizabeth, to which she replied, "Raleigh, when will you leave off begging?" "When Your Majesty leaves off giving," he replied. That is how long we must continue praying.

In an address he gave in Calcutta, George Müller said that five people were laid on his heart in 1844, and he began to pray for them. Eighteen months went by before one of them was converted. He prayed on for five more years, and another was converted. At the end of twelve and a half years, a third was converted. In addition, he had been praying for the other two for forty years without missing one single day for any reason whatsoever, but they were not yet converted. He felt encouraged, however, to continue in prayer, and he was sure of receiving an answer in relation to the two who were still resisting the Spirit.

Submission

Hear me, my God, and if my lip hath dared
    To murmur 'neath Thy hand, oh, teach me now
To feel each inmost thought before Thee bared,
    And this rebellious will in faith to bow.
Though I wept wildly o'er the ruined shrine,
    Where earthly idols held Thy place alone,
Now purify and make this temple Thine,
    And teach me, Lord, to say, "Thy will be done!"

What can I bring to offer that is mine?
    A youth of sorrow, and a life of sin.
What can I lay upon Thy hallowed shrine,
    One hope of pardon for the past to win?
While thus a suppliant at Thy feet I bow,
    Still dare I lift to Thee my tearful eyes,
I plead the promise of Thy word, that Thou
    A broken, contrite heart will not despise.

What shall I bring? A bruised spirit, Lord,
    Worn with the contest, pining now for rest,
And yearning for Thy peace, as some poor bird,
    'Mid the wild tempest, seeks its mother's breast,
My sacrifice, the Lamb who died for me;
    I plead the merits of Thy sinless Son;
I bring Thy promises; I trust in Thee;
    In love Thou smitest; Lord, "Thy will be done!"

—*Author Unknown*

CHAPTER 10

Submission

Another essential element in prayer is submission. All true prayer must be offered in full submission to God. After we have made our requests known to Him, our language should be, *"Thy will be done"* (Matt. 6:10). I would, a thousand times over, rather have God's will be done than my own. I cannot see into the future as God can; thus, it is far better to let Him choose for me than to choose for myself.

When it comes to spiritual matters, I know His will. For example, His will is that I should be sanctified; therefore, I can pray with confidence to God for that and expect an answer to my prayers. However, when it comes to temporal matters, it is different; what I ask for may not be God's purpose concerning me.

As one writer well put it,

> Depend upon it, prayer does not mean that I am to bring God down to my thoughts and my purposes and bend His government according to my foolish, silly, and sometimes sinful notions. Prayer means that I am to be raised up into feeling, into union and design with Him; that I

am to enter into His counsel and carry out His purpose fully. I am afraid that sometimes we think that prayer has an altogether opposite character—that by prayer we somehow persuade or influence our Father in heaven to do whatever comes into our own minds and whatever would accomplish our foolish, weak-sighted purposes. I am quite convinced of this, that God knows better what is best for me and for the world than I can possibly know; and even if it were in my power to say, "My will be done," I would rather say to Him, *"Thy will be done."*

I was told of a certain sick woman who was asked whether she wanted to live or die. She answered, "Whichever God pleases." "But," someone asked, "if God should give the matter to you to decide, which would you choose?" "Truly," she replied, "I would give it back to Him." Thus, we will obtain our will from God if our will is subjected to God.

Charles Spurgeon remarked on this subject,

> The believing man resorts to God at all times, that he may keep up his fellowship with the divine mind. Prayer is not a soliloquy, but a dialogue; not an introspection, but a looking toward the hills, from whence comes our help (Ps. 121:1). There is a relief in unburdening the mind to a sympathetic friend, and faith feels this abundantly; but there is more than this in prayer. When an obedient activity has been done to the fullest extent, and yet the needful thing is not reached, then the hand of God is trusted in

to go beyond us, just as before it was relied upon to go with us.

Faith has no desire to have its own will when that will is not in accordance with the mind of God. Such a desire would, at the core of it, be the impulse of an unbelief that did not rely upon God's judgment as our best guide. Faith knows that God's will is the highest good and anything that is beneficial to us will be granted to our petitions.

History informs us that when the Tusculani, a people of Italy, offended the infinitely more powerful Romans, Camillus, at the head of a considerable army, started on his march to subdue them. Conscious of their inability to cope with such an enemy, the Tusculani took the following method to appease him. They declined all thoughts of resistance, opened their gates, and every man applied himself to his proper business, resolving to submit where they knew it was in vain to contend.

Camillus, entering their city, was struck with the wisdom and candor of their conduct. The chief magistrate said to him, "We have so sincerely repented of our former folly that, in confidence that our repentance will satisfy a generous enemy, we are not afraid to acknowledge our fault." Then Camillus addressed himself to the people with these words: "You only, of all people, have found out the true method of abating the Roman fury, and your submission has proved your best defense. Upon these terms, we cannot find in our hearts to injure you any more than you could have found power to oppose us."

In view of the difficulty of bringing our hearts to this complete submission to the divine will, we may well adopt Fénelon's prayer: "O God, take my heart, for I cannot give it; and when Thou have it, keep it, for I cannot keep it for Thee; and save me in spite of myself."

Some of the best men the world has ever seen have made great mistakes on this point. Moses could pray for Israel and could prevail with God, but God did not answer the prayer that he made for himself. He asked that God would take him over the Jordan River so that he might see Lebanon. (See Deuteronomy 3:25.) After the forty years' wandering in the wilderness, he desired to go into the Promised Land. However, the Lord did not grant his desire. Was that a sign that God did not love him? By no means! He was a man greatly beloved of God, like Daniel, and yet God did not answer this prayer of his.

Your child says, "I want this or that," but you do not grant the request, because you know that it is the ruin of children to give them everything they want. Moses asked to enter the Promised Land, but the Lord had something else in store for him. As someone has said, "God kissed away his soul and took him home to Himself." God buried him (see Deuteronomy 34:5–6)—the greatest honor ever paid to mortal man.

Fifteen hundred years afterward, God answered the prayer of Moses. He allowed him to go into the Promised Land and get a glimpse of the coming glory. On the Mount of Transfiguration, with the great prophet Elijah and with Peter, James, and John, Moses heard the voice come from the throne of God, *"This is my beloved Son, in whom I am well pleased; hear ye him"* (Matt. 17:5). That was better than to have gone over the Jordan River, as Joshua did, and to have lived for thirty years in the land of Canaan. So, when our prayers for earthly things are not answered, let us submit to the will of God and know that it is all right.

When one inquired of a deaf and dumb boy why he thought he was born deaf and dumb, taking the chalk, he wrote on the board, *"Even so, Father: for so it seemed good in thy sight"* (Matt. 11:26).

John Brown, of Haddington, once said,

> No doubt I have met with trials like others; but yet so kind has God been to me that I think if He were to give me as many years as I have lived in the world, I would not desire one single circumstance in my lot changed, except that I wish there had been less sin. It might be written on my coffin, "Here lies one of the cares of Providence, who early lost both father and mother, and yet never wanted for the care of either."

Elijah was mighty in prayer; he brought fire down from heaven on his sacrifice, and his petitions brought rain on the thirsty land. He stood fearlessly before King Ahab in the power of prayer, yet we find him sitting under a juniper tree like a coward, asking God to let him die. (See 1 Kings 19:4.) The Lord loved him too much for that; He was going to take him up to heaven using a chariot of fire. Accordingly, we must not allow the devil to take advantage of us and make us believe that God does not love us because He does not grant all our petitions in the time and way we would have Him to.

Even as Moses takes up more room in the Old Testament than any other character, so it is with Paul in the New Testament, perhaps with the exception of the Lord Himself. Still, Paul did not know how to pray for himself. He implored the Lord to take away the *"thorn in the flesh"* (2 Cor. 12:7). His request was not granted, but the Lord bestowed upon him a greater blessing. He gave him more grace. (See 2 Corinthians 12:8–9.)

It may be we have some trial, some thorn in the flesh. If it is not God's will to take it away, let us ask Him to give us more grace in order to bear it. We find that Paul gloried in his setbacks and his infirmities, because the power of God rested upon him even more (2 Cor. 12:9). It may be that some of us feel as though everything is against us. May God give us grace to take Paul's platform and say, *"All things work together for good to them that love God"* (Rom. 8:28). So, when we pray to God, we must be submissive and say, *"Thy will be done"* (Matt. 6:10).

In the gospel of John we read, *"If ye"* (that *"if"* is a mountain to begin with), *"If ye abide in me, and my words abide in you, ye shall ask what ye will, and it shall be done unto you"* (John 15:7). The latter part is often quoted, but not the first part. Why, there is very little abiding in Christ nowadays! Many Christians go and visit Him once in a while, and that is all.

If Christ abides in my heart, of course I will not ask anything that is against His will. Further, how many of us have God's Word abiding in us? We must have authorization for our prayers. If we have some great desire, we must search the Scriptures to find if it is right to ask for it. Many things we want are not good for us, and many other things that we desire to avoid are really our best blessings.

A friend of mine was shaving one morning, and his little boy, not four years old, asked him for his razor and said he wanted to whittle with it. When the boy was told he could not have it, he began to cry as if his heart would break. I am afraid that there are many of us who are praying for razors.

John Bunyan, author of *The Pilgrim's Progress,* blessed God for that Bedford jail more than for anything else that happened to him in this life. We never pray for affliction, yet it is often the best thing we could ask.

Dyer said,

> Afflictions are blessings to us when we can bless God for afflictions. Suffering has kept many from sinning. God had one Son without sin, but He never had any without sorrow. Fiery trials make golden Christians; sanctified afflictions are spiritual promotions.

Rutherford wrote beautifully about the value of sanctified trial and the wisdom of submitting in it to God's will:

> Oh, what owe I to the file, to the hammer, to the furnace of my Lord Jesus, who has now let me see how good the wheat of Christ is that goes through His mill and His

oven, to be made bread for His own table! Grace tried is better than grace, and it is more than grace; it is glory in its infancy. I now see that godliness is more than external appearances and outward finery. Who knows the truth of grace without a trial? Oh, how little does Christ get of us, but that which He wins with much toil and great pains!

What is more, how soon faith would freeze without a cross! How many dumb crosses have been laid on my back, which never had a tongue to speak of the sweetness of Christ as this one has! When Christ blesses His own crosses with a tongue, they breathe out His love, wisdom, kindness, and care for us. Why should I shrink from the plow of my Lord, which makes deep furrows on my soul? I know that He is no idle husbandman; He purposes to have a crop. Oh, that this white, withered field were made fertile to bear a crop for Him, by whom it is so painfully cultivated, and that this fallow ground were broken up!

Why was I (such a fool!) grieved that He put His garland and His rose on my head— the glory and honor of His faithful witnesses? I desire now to make no more pleas with Christ. Truly He has not put me at a loss by what I suffer; He owes me nothing; for in my bonds how sweet and comfortable have the thoughts of Him been to me, wherein I find a sufficient recompense of reward! How blind are my adversaries who sent me to a banqueting house, to a house of wine, to the lovely feasts of my lovely

Lord Jesus, and not to a prison or place of exile!

We may close our remarks on this subject by a reference to the words of the prophet Jeremiah, in Lamentations, where he said,

The LORD is good unto them that wait for him, to the soul that seeketh him. It is good that a man should both hope and quietly wait for the salvation of the LORD. It is good for a man that he bear the yoke in his youth. He sitteth alone and keepeth silence, because he hath borne it upon him. He putteth his mouth in the dust; if so be there may be hope. He giveth his cheek to him that smiteth him: he is filled full with reproach. For the Lord will not cast off for ever: but though he cause grief, yet will he have compassion according to the multitude of his mercies. For he doth not afflict willingly nor grieve the children of men....Who is he that saith, and it cometh to pass, when the Lord commandeth it not? Out of the mouth of the most High proceedeth not evil and good? Wherefore doth a living man complain, a man for the punishment of his sins? Let us search and try our ways, and turn again to the LORD. Let us lift up our heart with our hands unto God in the heavens. (Lam. 3:25–33, 37–41)

The Hour of Prayer

Lord, what a change within us one short hour
    Spent in Thy presence will prevail to make!
    What heavy burdens from our bosoms take;
What parched grounds refresh as with a shower.

We kneel—and all around us seems to lower;
    We rise—and all, the distant and the near,
    Stands forth in sunny outline brave and clear;
We kneel—how weak! We rise—how full of power!

Why, therefore, should we do ourselves this wrong,
    Or others—that we are not always strong?
That we are ever overborne with care;
    That we should ever weak or heartless be,
    Anxious or troubled, while with us is prayer,
And joy, and strength, and courage, are with Thee?

                —Trench

CHAPTER 11

Answered Prayers

I n the gospel of John, we find out whose prayers are answered: *"If ye abide in me, and my words abide in you, ye shall ask what ye will, and it shall be done unto you"* (John 15:7). Now in James's epistle, we read of those whose prayers are not answered: *"Ye ask, and receive not, because ye ask amiss"* (James 4:3). There are many prayers not answered because we do not have the right motive; we have not complied with the Word of God; we ask amiss. It is a good thing that our prayers are not answered when we ask amiss. Our prayers also go unanswered when we do not pray according to the Scriptures. However, let us not be discouraged, or give up praying, although our prayers are not answered in the way we want them to be.

A man once went to George Müller and said he wanted him to pray for a certain thing. The man stated that he had asked God many, many times to grant him his request, but God had not seen fit to do it. Mr. Müller took out his notebook and showed the man the name of a person for whom, he said, he had prayed for twenty-four years. Mr. Müller added that the prayer had not been answered yet; but the Lord had given him assurance that the person was going to be converted, and his faith rested there.

We sometimes find that the answers to our prayers are delayed; at other times our prayers are answered right away while we are praying. Especially when men pray for mercy, how quickly the answer comes! Look at Paul when he cried, *"Lord, what wilt thou have me to do?"* (Acts 9:6). The answer came at once. The publican who went up to the temple to pray—he got an immediate answer. (See Luke 18:13–14.) The thief on the cross prayed, *"Lord, remember me when thou comest into thy kingdom!"* (Luke 23:42), and the answer came immediately, then and there. There are many cases of a similar kind in the Bible, but there are also others who prayed long and often.

The Lord delights in hearing us, His children, make our requests known to Him—telling all our troubles to Him. After we have prayed, we should wait for His time, because we do not know when that is.

There was a mother in Connecticut who had a son in the army, and it almost broke her heart when he left because he was not a Christian. Day after day, she lifted up her voice in prayer for her boy. She afterward learned that he had been taken to the hospital where he had died, but she could not find out anything about his spiritual condition when he had died.

Years passed, and one day a friend came to see some member of the family on business. There was a picture of the soldier boy on the wall. He looked at it and said, "Did you know that young man?" The mother said, "That young man was my son. He died in the war." The man replied, "I knew him very well; he was in my company." The mother then asked, "Do you know anything about his end?" The man said, "I was in the hospital, and he died a most peaceful death, triumphant in the faith." The mother had given up hope of ever hearing about her boy, but before she died, she had the satisfaction of knowing that her prayers had prevailed with God.

When we get to heaven, I think we will find that many of our prayers that we thought had gone unanswered truly were answered. If our prayer is the true prayer of faith, God will not disappoint us. Let us not doubt God.

On one occasion, at a meeting I attended, a gentleman pointed out an individual and said, "Do you see that man over there? He is one of the leaders of an infidel club." I sat down beside him, and the infidel said, "I am not a Christian. You have been deceiving these people long enough and making some of these old women believe that you get answers to prayer. Try it on me." I prayed, and when I got up, the infidel said with a good deal of sarcasm, "I am not converted; God has not answered your prayer!" I said, "But you may be converted yet." Some time afterward I received a letter from a friend, stating that he had been converted and was at work in the meetings.

Jeremiah prayed and said,

Ah Lord GOD! behold, thou hast made the heaven and the earth by thy great power and stretched out arm, and there is nothing too hard for thee. (Jer. 32:17)

Nothing is too hard for God; that is a good thing to take for a motto. I believe this is a time of great blessing in the world, and we may expect great things. While the blessing is falling all around, let us arise and share in it. God has said, *"Call unto me, and I will answer thee, and show thee great and mighty things, which thou knowest not"* (Jer. 33:3). Now let us call on the Lord, and let us pray that it may be done for Christ's sake—not our own.

At a Christian convention a number of years ago, a leading man got up and spoke—his subject being "For Christ's Sake"—and he shed new light on that passage. I had never before heard it the way he put it. When the war broke out, this gentleman's only son had enlisted, and the gentleman never saw a company of soldiers without his heart going out to them. A soldiers' home was started in the city where he lived, and he gladly joined the committee and acted as president.

Some time afterward, he said to his wife, "I have given so much time to these soldiers that I have neglected my business," and he went down to his office with the fixed determination that he would not be disturbed by any soldiers that day. The door opened soon after, and he saw a soldier entering. He paid no attention to him but kept on writing; and the poor fellow stood for some time.

At last the soldier put before him a soiled piece of paper that had some writing on it. The gentleman observed that it was the handwriting of his son, Charlie, and he seized the letter at once and read it. It was something to this effect: "Dear father, this young man belongs to my company. He has lost his health in defense of his country, and he is on his way home to his mother to die. Treat him kindly for Charlie's sake."

The gentleman at once dropped his work and took the soldier to his house, where he was kindly cared for until he was able to be sent home to his mother. Then he took him to the station and sent him home with a "God bless you, for Charlie's sake!"

Let our prayers, then, be for Christ's sake. If we want our sons and daughters converted, let us pray that it be done for Christ's sake. If that is the motive, our prayers will be answered. If God gave up Christ for the world, what will He not give us? (See Romans 8:32.) If He gave Christ to the murderers, blasphemers, and the rebels of a world lying in wickedness and sin, what would He not give to those who go to Him for Christ's sake? Let our prayer be that God may advance His work, not for our glory—not for our sake—but for the sake of His beloved Son whom He has sent. Furthermore, let us remember that when we pray we ought to expect an answer. Let us be looking for it.

At the close of a meeting in one of the Southern cities near the end of the Civil War, a man came up to me weeping and trembling. I thought something I had said had touched him, and I began to question him as to what it was. I found, however, that he could not repeat a word of what I had said. "My friend," I said, "what is the trouble?" He put his hand into his pocket and brought out a letter, all soiled, as if his tears had fallen on it.

"I got that letter," he said, "from my sister last night. She tells me that every night she kneels down and prays to God for me. I think I am the worst man in all the army of the Cumberland. I have been perfectly wretched today." That sister was six hundred miles away, but she had brought her brother to his knees in answer to her earnest, believing prayer. It was a hard case, but God heard and answered the prayer of this godly sister, so that the man was as clay in the hands of the Potter. He was soon brought into the kingdom of God—all through his sister's prayers.

I traveled some thirty miles to another place, where I told this story. A young man, a lieutenant in the army, sprang to his feet and said, "That reminds me of the last letter I got from my mother. She told me that every night as the sun went down she prayed for me. She begged of me, when I got her letter, to go away alone and yield myself to God. I put the letter in my pocket, thinking there would be plenty of time." He went on to say that the next news that came from home was that his mother was gone. He went out into the woods alone and cried to his mother's God to have mercy upon him. As he stood in the meeting with his face shining, that lieutenant said, "My mother's prayers are answered, and my only regret is that she did not live to know it; but I will meet her in heaven." So, although we may not live to see the answer to our prayers, if we cry mightily to God, the answer will come.

In Scotland, many years ago, there lived a man with his wife and three children—two girls and a boy. He was in the habit of getting drunk and then losing his job. At last he said he would take little Johnny and go off to America, where he would be away from his old associates and

144

where he could commence life over again. He took the little fellow, seven years old, and went away. Soon after he arrived in America, he went into a saloon and got drunk. He got separated from his boy in the streets, and the man has never been seen by his friends since. The little fellow was placed in an institution and afterward apprenticed in Massachusetts.

After he had been there some time, he became discontented and went off to sea; finally, he came to Chicago to work on the lakes. He had been a roving spirit, had gone over sea and land, and now he was in Chicago. When the vessel came into port one time, he was invited to a gospel meeting. The joyful sound of the Good News reached him, and he became a Christian.

After he had been a Christian a little while, he became very anxious to find his mother. He wrote to different places in Scotland but could not find out where she was. One day he read in the Psalms, *"No good thing will he withhold from them that walk uprightly"* (Ps. 84:11). He closed his Bible, got down on his knees, and said, "O God, I have been trying to walk uprightly for months past; help me to find my mother."

It came into his mind to write back to the place in Massachusetts from which he had run away years before. It turned out that a letter from Scotland had been waiting for him there for seven years. He wrote at once to the place in Scotland and found that his mother was still living; the answer came back immediately. I wish you could have seen him when he got that letter. He brought it to me, and the tears flowed so that he could scarcely read it. His sister had written

on behalf of their mother; she had been so over-
come by the tidings of her long-lost boy that she
could not write.

His sister said that all the nineteen years he
had been away, his mother had prayed to God
day and night that he might be saved, and that
she might live to know what had become of him
and to see him once more. Now, said the sister,
she was overjoyed, not only that he was alive,
but even more that he had become a Christian. It
was not long before the mother and sisters came
out to Chicago to meet him.

I mention this incident to show how God answers prayer. This mother cried to God for nineteen long years. It must have seemed to her
sometimes as though God did not intend to give
her the desire of her heart; nonetheless, she kept
praying, and at last the answer came.

The following personal testimony was pub-
licly given at one of our meetings lately held in
London. It may serve to help and encourage
readers of these pages.

A Prayer Meeting Testimony

"I want you to understand, my friends, that
what I am about to tell is not what I did, but
what God did. Only God could have done it! I had
given it up as a bad job long before. However, it
is of God's great mercy that I am still alive to tell
you that Christ is able to save *to the uttermost* all
that come to God through Him (Heb. 7:25).

"When prayer requests are made for the salvation of inebriates, I am touched very deeply.
They seem to be an echo of many a request for

146

prayer that had been made for me. From my knowledge of society generally, and of human nature, I know that in many, many families there is need of some such request.

"Therefore, if what I tell you will cheer any Christian heart, encourage any godly father and mother to go on praying for their sons, or assist any man or woman who has felt himself or herself beyond the reach of hope, I will thank God for it.

"I had very good opportunities in my youth. My parents loved the Lord Jesus and did their best to train me up in the right path, and for some time I myself thought that I should be a Christian. However, I got away from Christ; I turned away from God and all good influences.

"It was at a public school that I first learned to drink. Many a time at seventeen I drank to excess, but I had an amount of self-respect that kept me from giving myself thoroughly to evil, until I was about twenty-three; but from then until I was twenty-six, I went steadily downhill. At Cambridge, I drank more and more until I lost all self-respect and voluntarily chose the worst of companions.

"I strayed further and further from God, until my friends, those who were Christians and those who were not, considered and told me that there was very little hope for me. I had been pleaded with by all sorts of people, but I 'hated reproof.' (See Proverbs 12:1; 15:10.) I hated everything that smacked of religion, and I sneered at every bit of good advice or any kind word offered me by a religious person.

"My father and mother both died without seeing me brought to the Lord. They prayed for

me all the time they lived, and at the very last my
mother asked me if I would not follow her to be
with her by and by in heaven. To quiet and
soothe her, I said I would. However, I did not
mean it; and I thought, when she had passed
away, that she then knew my real feelings. After
her death, I went from bad to worse and plunged
deeper and deeper into vice. Drink got a stronger
hold of me, and I went lower and lower down. I
was never 'in the gutter,' in the generally under-
stood meaning of the term, but I was as low in
my soul as any man who lives in one of the sinful
lodging houses.

"I left Cambridge to go, first, to a town in the
north, where I was apprenticed to a lawyer, and
then I went to London. While I was in the north,
Mr. Moody and Mr. Sankey came to the town
where I lived. An aunt of mine, who was still
praying for me after my mother's death, came
and said to me, 'I have a favor to ask of you.' She
had been very kind to me, but I knew what she
wanted. She said, 'I want you to go and hear Mr.
Moody and Mr. Sankey.' 'Very good,' I said, 'it is
a bargain. I will go and hear the men, but you
are never to ask me again. Will you promise
that?' 'Yes,' she said, 'I do promise.' I went, and
most religiously kept, as I thought, my share of
the bargain.

"I waited until the sermon was over, and I
saw Mr. Moody coming down from the pulpit.
Earnest prayer had been offered for me, and
there had been an understanding between my
aunt and him that the sermon should apply to
me and that he would come and speak to me
immediately afterward. We met Mr. Moody in the

148

aisle, and I thought that I had done a very clever thing when, before Mr. Moody could address me, I walked around my aunt and out of the building.

"I wandered further from God after that, and I do not think that I bent my knees in prayer for between two and three years. When I went to London, things grew worse and worse. At times I tried to change my ways. I made any number of resolutions. I promised myself and my friends I would not touch alcohol. I kept my resolutions for a few days, and, on one occasion, for six months; but the temptation came with stronger force than ever and swept me further and further from the pathway of virtue. When in London, I neglected my business and everything I ought to have done and sank deeper into sin.

"One of my jovial friends said to me, 'If you don't change your ways, you will kill yourself.' 'How is that?' I asked. 'You are killing yourself,' he said, 'for you can't drink so much as you used to.' 'Well,' I replied, 'I can't help it, then.' I got to such a state that I did not think there was any possible help for me.

"The description of these things pains me, and as I relate them, God forbid that I should feel anything but shame. I am telling you these things because we have a Savior, and if the Lord Jesus Christ saved even me, He is able also to save you.

"Affairs went on in this manner until, at last, I lost all control of myself.

"I had been drinking and playing billiards one day, and in the evening I returned to my lodgings. I thought that I would sit there awhile and then go out again, as usual. Before going out, I began to think, and the thought struck me, 'How will all this end?' 'Oh,' I thought to myself, 'what is the use of thinking about that? I know how it will end—in my eternal destruction, body and soul!' I felt I was killing my body, and I knew too well what would be the result to my soul. I thought it impossible for me to be saved. However, the thought came to me very strongly, 'Is there any way of escape?' 'No,' I said, 'I have made any number of resolutions. I have done all I could to keep clear of drink, but I can't. It is impossible.'

"Just at that moment the words came into my mind, from God's own Word—words that I had not remembered since I was a boy: '*With men this is impossible; but with God all things are possible*' (Matt. 19:26). Then I saw in a flash that what I had just admitted, as I had hundreds of times before, to be impossible, was the one thing that God had pledged Himself to do if I would go to Him. All the difficulties that stood in my way came to mind: my companions, my surroundings, and my temptations; but I just looked up and thought, 'It is possible with God.'

"I went down on my knees there and then, in my room, and began to ask God to do the impossible. As soon as I prayed to Him, with very stammering utterance—I had not prayed for nearly three years—I thought, 'Now, then, God will help me.' I took hold of His truth, although I didn't know how. It was nine days before I knew how and before I had any assurance, peace, or rest in my soul. Nevertheless, I got up at that point with the hope that God would save me. I took it to be the truth, and I ultimately proved it, for which I praise God.

"I thought the best thing I could do would be to go and get somebody to talk to me about my soul and tell me how to be saved, for I was a perfect heathen, although I had been brought up well. I went out and hunted about London, and it shows how little I knew of religious people and places of worship that I could not find a Wesleyan chapel. My mother and father were Wesleyans, and I thought I would find a place belonging to their denomination, but I could not. I searched an hour and a half, and that night I was in the most abject, utter misery of body and soul that any man can imagine.

"I came home to my lodgings and went upstairs, and I thought to myself, 'I will not go to bed until I am saved.' However, I was very ill from drinking—I had not had my usual amount of food in the evening, and the reaction was so tremendous that I felt I must go to bed (although I dared not), or I would be in a very serious condition in the morning.

"I knew how I would be in the morning, thinking, 'What a fool I was last night!' when I would wake up moderately fresh; then I would go off to drink again, as I had often done. However, I thought, 'God can do the impossible. He will do what I cannot do myself.' And I prayed to the Lord to let me wake up in much the same condition as that in which I went to bed, feeling the weight of my sins and my misery. Then I went to sleep. The first thing in the morning, as soon as I remembered where I was, I thought, 'Has the conviction left me?' No, I was more miserable than before, and—it seemed strange, though it was natural—I got up and thanked the Lord because He had kept me anxious about my soul.

"Have you ever felt like that? Perhaps after some meeting or conversation with some Christian, or after reading the Word of God, you have gone to your room, miserable and 'almost persuaded.' (See Acts 26:28.)

"I went on for eight or nine days seeking the Lord. On the Saturday morning I had to go and tell my friends. That was hard. I did it with tears running down my cheeks. A man does not like to cry in front of other men. Anyway, I told them I wanted to become, and meant to become, a Christian. The Lord helped me with that promise, 'With God all things are possible' (Matt. 19:26).

"One friend, a skeptic, dropped his head and said nothing. Another fellow, with whom I played billiards, said, 'I wish I had the courage to say so myself!' My words were received in a different way from what I thought they would be. However, the very man who had told me that I was killing myself with drink, spent an hour and a half trying to get me to drink, saying that I 'had the blues and was out of sorts, and that a glass of brandy or whisky would do me good.' He tried to get me to drink, and I turned upon him at last and said, 'You remember what you said to me; I am trying to get away from drink and to never touch it again.' When I think of that I am reminded of the words of God Himself: 'The tender mercies of the wicked are cruel' (Prov. 12:10).

"The Lord drew me on until the little thread became a cable by which my soul could swing. He drew me nearer until I found that He was my

Savior. Truly He is able *'to save them to the utter-most that come unto God by him'* (Heb. 7:25).

"I must not forget to tell you that I knelt before God in my misery, my helplessness, and my sin, and acknowledged to Him that it was impossible for me to save myself, that it was impossible for me to keep clear of drink. However, from that night to this moment, I have never had the slightest desire for drink.

"It was a hard struggle indeed to give up smoking. However, God, in His great wisdom, knew that I would have come to grief if I had had to fight single-handedly against the overwhelming desire I had for drink; and He took that desire completely away. From that day to this, the Lord has kept me away from drink and has made me hate it most bitterly. I simply said that I did not have any strength—nor do I have any now—but it is the Lord Jesus who is *'able also to save them to the uttermost that come unto God by him.'*

"If there is anyone who has given up all hope, come to the Savior! That is His name, *'for he shall save his people from their sins'* (Matt. 1:21). Wherever I have gone since then, I have found Him to be my Savior. God forbid that I should glory! It would be glorying in my shame. It is to my shame that I speak thus of myself, but, oh, the Savior is able to save, and He will save!

"Christian friends, continue to pray. You may go to heaven before your sons are brought home. My parents did, and my sisters prayed for me for years and years. However, now I can help others on their way to Zion. Praise the Lord for all His mercy to me!

"Remember, *'with God all things are possible'* (Matt. 19:26). And then you may say, along with the apostle Paul, *'I can do all things through Christ which strengtheneth me'* (Phil. 4:13)."

⌘⌘⌘⌘⌘

Yes, Christian friends, keep praying, and look up, even as this poem bids us:

Look Up

O soul most desolate, look up! For thee
One faithful voice doth promise sure relief.
Whate'er thy sin, whate'er thy sorrow be,
Tell all to Jesus. He looketh where
The weary-hearted weep, and draweth near
To listen fondly to the half-formed prayer,
Or read the silent pleading of a tear.
Lose not thy privilege, O silent soul;
Pour out thy sorrow at thy Savior's feet.
What outcast spurns the hand that gives the dole?
Oh, let Him hear thy voice; to Him thy voice is
    sweet.

—A. S.

About the Author

On February 5, 1837, in Northfield, Massachusetts, Dwight Lyman Moody was born, the sixth in what would be a family of nine children. His father died when Moody was only a tender child, leaving little provision for the family. Hence, Moody learned the value of hard work at an early age. An ambitious Moody went to Boston at the age of seventeen, where he became a successful salesman in his uncle's shoe store. His uncle made him promise to go to church, a promise that he faithfully kept, and he was won to the Lord by his Sunday school teacher.

In 1856 Moody went to Chicago, where he continued to succeed as a shoe salesman. His fervor in selling shoes was exceeded, however, by his zeal in winning souls, and he began to pack the pews of the church with young men. At the age of twenty-three, he devoted himself to full-time Christian work. Because of his poor grammar, his first attempts at public speaking were not well received by all; one deacon told him that he would serve God best by keeping still. Nonetheless, Moody persevered, and he became famous nationwide for his Sunday school work. He was also known for his work among the soldiers during the Civil War; many were brought to

Christ through his meetings and through his distribution of Bibles and tracts.

In 1867, Moody traveled to Great Britain to learn new methods in Christian work. It was there that his heart was stirred and forever changed by these words: "The world has yet to see what God will do with...the man who is fully consecrated to Him." Moody determined to be that man.

For Moody, the road of total commitment was not all smooth and straight. In 1871, the church that Moody pastored, the largest church in Chicago, was destroyed in the Chicago fire. However, in the wake of this disaster, Moody received the filling of the Holy Spirit. Never before had he experienced such a mighty revelation of God's love.

After this empowering of the Spirit, Moody went on to accomplish even more for Christ. He held meetings in America, England, and Scotland, where thousands were in attendance and many were brought to Christ.

When Moody died in 1899, he left a rich legacy: three Christian schools, a Christian publishing business, and a million souls won for Christ! The day of his death was not a sad day; rather, Moody exclaimed, "This is my triumph; this is my coronation day!"

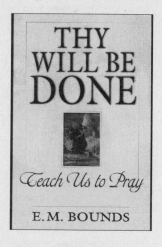